OFFICIAL
Instant Pot
BOOK

The "I LOVE MY INSTANT POT®" Soups, Stews, and Chilis

Recipe Book

From *Chicken Noodle Soup* to *Lobster Bisque*, 175 Easy and Delicious Recipes

Kelly Jaggers

Author of *The Everything® Easy Instant Pot® Cookbook*

Adams Media

New York   London   Toronto   Sydney   New Delhi

Adams Media
An Imprint of Simon & Schuster, Inc.
57 Littlefield Street
Avon, Massachusetts 02322

First Adams Media trade paperback edition December 2019

ADAMS MEDIA and colophon are trademarks of Simon & Schuster.

For information about special discounts for bulk purchases, please contact Simon & Schuster Special Sales at 1-866-506-1949 or business@simonandschuster.com.

The Simon & Schuster Speakers Bureau can bring authors to your live event. For more information or to book an event contact the Simon & Schuster Speakers Bureau at 1-866-248-3049 or visit our website at www.simonspeakers.com.

Interior design by Colleen Cunningham
Interior layout by Julia Jacintho
Photographs by Kelly Jaggers
Nutritional analysis by Melinda Boyd

Manufactured in the United States of America

10 9 8 7 6 5 4 3 2 1

Library of Congress Cataloging-in-Publication Data
Names: Jaggers, Kelly, author.
Title: The "I love my instant pot®" soups, stews, and chilis recipe book / Kelly Jaggers, author of The everything® easy instant pot® cookbook.
Description: Avon, Massachusetts: Adams Media, 2019.
Series: "I love my" series.
Includes index.
Identifiers: LCCN 2019039412 | ISBN 9781507212288 (pb) | ISBN 9781507212295 (ebook)
Subjects: LCSH: Pressure cooking. | Electric cooking. | LCGFT: Cookbooks.
Classification: LCC TX840.P7 J35 2019 | DDC 641.5/86--dc23
LC record available at https://lccn.loc.gov/2019039412

ISBN 978-1-5072-1228-8
ISBN 978-1-5072-1229-5 (ebook)

Always follow safety and commonsense cooking protocols while using kitchen utensils, operating ovens and stoves, and handling uncooked food. If children are assisting in the preparation of any recipe, they should always be supervised by an adult.

Contains material adapted from the following titles published by Adams Media, an Imprint of Simon & Schuster, Inc.: *The Everything® Easy Instant Pot® Cookbook* by Kelly Jaggers, copyright © 2018, ISBN 978-1-5072-0940-0, and *The "I Love My Instant Pot®" Recipe Book* by Michelle Fagone, copyright © 2017, ISBN 978-1-5072-0228-9.

Contents

and free from grease or other food debris. The steam release is next to the float valve. It is a plastic knob that should rotate easily from Sealing to Venting. Be careful when turning the knob to avoid a steam burn. Keep your fingers, arms, and face away from the steam when you manually release pressure.

Condensation Collector

There is a condensation collector on the side of the machine. It catches and holds condensation while your Instant Pot® is coming up to pressure. It snaps on and off the machine easily so it can be drained and cleaned.

Inner Pot

The inner pot is where the magic happens! It should be dent-free, fit snugly in the body of the machine, and have a high shine. The inner pot has measurement lines to make it easy to gauge the volume of food or liquid in the pot. The inner pot can be cleaned in the dishwasher or hand-washed with mild detergent and a soft scrubbing sponge. Make sure that the inner pot is completely clean and dry before inserting it into the machine.

Power Cord

The Instant Pot® comes with a power cord that is short in length to prevent the machine from getting pulled or dragged, or the cord from becoming tangled. The plug is a three-pronged grounded plug and should be used with a grounded outlet. The power cord should never be allowed to hang off the edge of a counter, and you should not use your Instant Pot® with an extension cord.

Function Buttons

You are staring at the Instant Pot® and there are so many buttons. Which one should you use? Although most of the function buttons seem obvious, several are set at preprogrammed default cooking times. And for every option, the Instant Pot® starts cooking 10 seconds after you hit the button. Mostly likely, you will utilize the Manual button the most because you are in complete control, but read on for more detailed information on the remaining function buttons.

Manual Button

This might be your most used button on the Instant Pot®. The default pressure setting is High; however, you can toggle the pressure from High to Low by pressing the Pressure button. Use the Plus and Minus buttons to adjust the pressurized cooking time.

Sauté Button

This button helps the Instant Pot® act as a skillet for sautéing vegetables or searing meat prior to adding the remaining ingredients of a recipe, and it is used for simmering sauces as well. There are three temperature settings—Normal, Less, and More—that can be accessed using the Adjust button. The Normal setting is for sautéing, the Less setting is for simmering, and the More setting is for searing meat. Keep the lid open when using the Sauté button to avoid pressure building up.

Soup Button

This button is used to cook soups and broths at high pressure for a default of 30 minutes. The Adjust button allows you to change the cooking time to 20 or 40 minutes.

Porridge Button

This button is used to cook porridge, congee, and jook at high pressure for a default of 20 minutes. The Adjust button allows you to change the cooking time to 15 or 40 minutes.

Poultry Button

This button is used to cook chicken, turkey, and even duck at high pressure for a default of 15 minutes. The Adjust button allows you to change the cooking time to 5 or 30 minutes.

Meat/Stew Button

This button is used to cook red meats and chunky meat stews at high pressure for a default of 35 minutes. The Adjust button allows you to change the cooking time to 20 or 45 minutes.

Bean/Chili Button

This button is used to cook dried beans and chili at high pressure for a default of 30 minutes. The Adjust button allows you to change the cooking time to 25 or 40 minutes.

Rice Button

This button is used to cook white rice such as jasmine or basmati at low pressure. The Instant Pot® will automatically set the default cooking time by sensing the amount of water and rice that are in the cooking vessel.

Multigrain Button

This button is used to cook grains such as wild rice, quinoa, and barley at high pressure for a default of 40 minutes. The Adjust button allows you to change the cooking time to 20 or 60 minutes.

Steam Button

This button is excellent for steaming vegetables and seafood using your steamer basket. It steams for a default of 10 minutes. The Adjust button allows you to change the cooking time to 3 or 15 minutes. Quick-release the steam immediately after the timer beeps so as to not overcook the food.

Slow Cook Button

This button allows the Instant Pot® to cook like a slow cooker. It defaults to a 4-hour cook time. The Adjust button allows you to change the temperature to Less, Normal, or More, which correspond to a slow cooker's low, normal, or high settings. The Plus and Minus buttons allow you to manually adjust the cooking time.

Keep Warm/Cancel Button

When the Instant Pot® is being programmed or in operation, pressing this button cancels the operation and returns the Instant Pot® to a standby state. When the Instant Pot® is in the standby state, pressing this button again activates the Keep Warm function.

Automatic Keep Warm Function

After the ingredients in the Instant Pot® are finished cooking, the Instant Pot® automatically switches over to the Keep Warm function and will keep your food warm for up to 10 hours. This is perfect for large cuts of meat as well as soups, stews, and chilis, allowing the spices and flavors to really marry together for an even better taste. The first digit on the LED display will show an "L" to indicate that the Instant Pot® is in the Keep Warm cycle, and the clock will count up from 0 seconds to 10 hours.

Timer Button

This button allows you to delay the start of cooking up to 24 hours. After you select a cooking program and make any time adjustments, press the Timer button and use the Plus or Minus keys to enter the delayed hours; press the Timer button again and use the Plus or Minus keys to enter the delayed minutes. You can press the Keep Warm/Cancel button to cancel the timed delay. The Timer function doesn't work with Sauté, Yogurt, and Keep Warm functions.

Locking and Pressure Release Methods

Other than the Sauté function, where the lid should be off, or the Slow Cook or Keep Warm functions, where the lid can be on or off, most of the cooking you'll do in the Instant Pot® will be under pressure, which means you need to know how to lock the lid before pressurized cooking and how to safely release the pressure after cooking.

Once your ingredients are in the inner pot of the Instant Pot®, to lock the lid put the lid on the Instant Pot® with the triangle mark on the lid aligned with the Unlocked mark on the side of the Instant Pot® rim. Then turn the lid 30 degrees clockwise until the triangle mark on the lid is aligned with the Locked mark on the rim. Turn the pointed end of the pressure release knob on top of the lid to the Sealing position. After your cooking program has ended or you've pressed the Keep Warm/Cancel button to end the cooking, there are two ways you can release the pressure:

Natural-Release Method

To naturally release the pressure, simply wait until the Instant Pot® has cooled sufficiently for all of the pressure to be released and the float valve drops, normally about 10–15 minutes. You can either unplug the Instant Pot® while the pressure naturally releases or allow the pressure to release while it is still on the Keep Warm function.

Quick-Release Method

The quick-release method stifles the cooking process and helps unlock the lid for immediate serving. To quickly release the pressure on the Instant Pot®, make sure you are wearing oven mitts, then turn the pressure release handle to the Venting position to let out steam until the float valve drops. This is generally not recommended for starchy items or large volumes of liquids (e.g., soup) so as to avoid any splattering that may occur. Be prepared, because the noise and geyser effect of the releasing steam experienced during the quick-release method can be off-putting.

Also, if you have dogs, apparently this release is the most frightening part of their day so take caution.

Cleaning Your Instant Pot®

When cleaning up after use, the first thing you should do is unplug the Instant Pot® and allow it to cool. Then you can break down the following parts to clean and inspect for any trapped food particles:

Inner Pot

The inner pot, the cooking vessel, is dishwasher safe; however, the high heat causes rainbowing, or discoloration, on stainless steel. To avoid this, hand-wash the pot.

Outer Heating Unit

Wipe the interior and exterior with a damp cloth. Do not submerge in water, as it is an electrical appliance.

Lid

The lid needs to be broken down into individual parts before washing. The sealing ring, the float valve, the steam release handle, and the anti-block shield all need to be cleaned in different ways:

- **Sealing ring.** Once this ring is removed, check the integrity of the silicone. If this ring is torn or cracked, it will not seal properly and may cause a hindrance to the cooking process and should not be used. The sealing ring needs to be removed and washed each time because the ring has a tendency to hold odors when cooking. Vinegar or lemon juice are excellent for reducing the odors. For a nominal price, additional rings can be purchased. Some use one ring for meats and a separate one for desserts and milder dishes.
- **Float valve.** The float valve is a safety feature that serves as a latch lock that prevents the lid from being opened during the cooking process. Make sure that this valve can move easily and is not obstructed by any food particles.
- **Steam release handle.** This is the venting handle on top of the lid. It can be pulled out for cleaning. It should be loose so don't worry. This allows it to move when necessary.
- **Anti-block shield.** The anti-block shield is the little silver "basket" on the under side of the lid. It is located directly below the vent. This shield can and should be removed and cleaned. It blocks any foods, especially starches, so they don't clog the vent.

Getting the Most from Your Pressure Cooker

Once you get to know your Instant Pot®, you will be eager to start cooking. This section will cover some tips for success, including tips for getting maximum flavor from your foods, what to do when things don't come out quite like you expected, and how to ensure your dishes cook evenly. You will also learn how to convert time-tested family-favorite recipes to the Instant Pot®.

Prep Work

Foods cooked in a pressure cooker need to be prepared properly for the best results. Here are a few things to keep in mind. First, ensure the food you want to cook will fit into the pot. Larger pieces of meat should be cut into smaller, evenly sized pieces if needed. Smaller pieces cook more quickly, so you may need to adjust your cooking time accordingly. Second, vegetables of a similar density should be cut into similar sizes for even cooking. Also keep in mind that firm vegetables cook more slowly than soft vegetables, so cut the firm vegetables into smaller pieces than the softer ones. Third, brown meats and some types of vegetables directly in the pot to retain maximum flavor. Once you have finished browning your food, add a little of the cooking liquid to the hot pot and scrape up any browned bits to add even more flavor to the finished product. Finally, starchy foods like pasta, beans, barley, rice, and cereals can create foam while cooking, which can cause problems when manually releasing pressure. Adding a little fat, such as a tablespoon of olive oil or butter, to the pot helps keep foam to a minimum.

Troubleshooting Recipes

Once cooking is complete and the machine has safely released pressure, open the lid and check the food. Sometimes new recipes may take a little tweaking to get right, so don't be discouraged if things do not come out perfectly the first time out. For tough meat, hard beans, or undercooked vegetables, the easiest fix is to cook the food a little longer. Often 3–5 minutes more is all it takes, but meats may need another 10 minutes. Since the food is already hot, the time it needs to come to pressure will be reduced, so you won't have long to wait. For soups or gravies that are too thin, press the Sauté button and allow the liquid to reduce naturally, stirring often.

You can also quickly thicken pan juices and gravies by adding a cornstarch slurry. To every tablespoon of cornstarch add 3 tablespoons of water, mix well, and then stir into a simmering liquid. Cook until the liquid thickens, about 30 seconds.

Remember, when cooking under pressure it is best to err on the side of less time so your food is not overcooked. This is particularly true with pasta and grains. You can always add more cooking time, but you can't take it away.

Converting Recipes

When converting favorite recipes for the Instant Pot®, keep a few points in mind. First, verify that the amount of food you are cooking does not exceed the amount your model can hold. Second, be sure you have enough liquid to bring the machine to pressure. Usually ½ cup of liquid is enough. Third, determine your cooking time. The time charts included in your model's recipe book will help you figure out the right amount of time for both fresh and frozen foods. Another option is to try one of the programmed cooking functions. As stated before, err on the side of undercooking when trying out a new recipe.

Broth and Stock Basics

The foundation of a good soup, stew, or chili is a flavorful base: a well-made, hearty broth or stock. Sure, you can buy a box of broth or stock at the grocery store, but it is so much better, and more flavorful, when you make it yourself. Cooking broth and stock on the stove can take hours. When you use your Instant Pot®, you have an express pass to flavorful broths and stocks that can be used in your soup recipes and in so many other ways.

The magic of a good stock or broth is that it packs tons of flavor and is incredibly versatile. Feel a cold coming on? A steaming bowl of Chicken Broth will cure what ails you. Want to make a flavorful vegetarian risotto? Roasted Vegetable Stock is exactly what you need. Looking for a filling snack? A cup of Bone Broth will do the trick!

Clear broths and stocks can be made in advance and refrigerated for up to seven days or frozen for up to three months, meaning extra broth and stock never has to go to waste. One afternoon of stock or broth making can yield many delicious meals to come!

Chicken Broth

Chicken broth is traditionally quick to prepare, and the Instant Pot® makes it even faster.

- **Hands-On Time: 5 minutes**
- **Cook Time: 45 minutes**

Serves 8

1 (3½-pound) chicken
2 stalks celery, chopped
2 medium yellow onions, peeled and quartered
2 medium carrots, peeled and chopped
3 cloves garlic, peeled and crushed
1 bay leaf
2 sprigs fresh thyme
1 teaspoon (about 10) whole black peppercorns
1 sprig fresh sage
2 quarts water

1 Place all ingredients in the Instant Pot®. Close lid, set steam release to Sealing, press the Manual button, and set time to 45 minutes.

2 When the timer beeps, let pressure release naturally, about 30 minutes. Open lid. Carefully lift out chicken and reserve for another use. Strain broth into a jar and use immediately, refrigerate for up to seven days, or freeze for up to three months.

PER SERVING

CALORIES: 20 | FAT: 1g | PROTEIN: 2g | SODIUM: 8mg
FIBER: 0g | CARBOHYDRATES: 0g | SUGAR: 0g

Basic Cream Soup Base

This base is the perfect starting point for a creamy soup. Swap out the Chicken Broth for Vegetable Broth (see recipes in this chapter) for a vegetarian version.

- **Hands-On Time: 15 minutes**
- **Cook Time: 1 minute**

Serves 8

4 tablespoons unsalted butter
2 stalks celery, diced
½ medium yellow onion, peeled and diced
¼ cup all-purpose flour
½ teaspoon salt
4 cups Chicken Broth (see recipe in this chapter)
½ cup heavy whipping cream

1 Press the Sauté button on the Instant Pot® and melt butter. Add celery and onion. Sauté until soft, about 8 minutes. Add flour and salt and cook for 1 minute. Press the Cancel button.

2 Whisk in broth slowly. Close lid, set steam release to Sealing, press the Manual button, and set time to 1 minute.

3 When the timer beeps, quick-release the pressure. Open lid, press the Cancel button, then press the Sauté button. Cook, whisking constantly, until the desired thickness is achieved. Stir in cream. Use immediately.

PER SERVING

CALORIES: 120 | FAT: 11g | PROTEIN: 1g | SODIUM: 159mg
FIBER: 0g | CARBOHYDRATES: 4g | SUGAR: 1g

Beef Broth

The Instant Pot® helps you get every bit of flavor out of the beef and vegetables for a boldly flavored broth. You will also have a lot of beef left over that can be used for other recipes. Try it mixed with your favorite barbecue sauce for sliders.

- **Hands-On Time: 10 minutes**
- **Cook Time: 1 hour**

Serves 8

1 tablespoon olive oil

1 pound chuck or round beef, cut into 3" pieces

1 teaspoon sea salt

2 stalks celery, cut into 2" pieces

1 medium white onion, peeled and quartered

1 medium carrot, peeled and cut into 2" pieces

4 cloves garlic, peeled and crushed

1 tablespoon tomato paste

2 sprigs fresh thyme or ½ teaspoon dried thyme

2 sprigs fresh oregano or ½ teaspoon dried oregano

1 teaspoon (about 10) whole black peppercorns

2 quarts water

1. Press the Sauté button on the Instant Pot® and heat oil. Season beef with salt and brown well on all sides, about 5 minutes per side. Press the Cancel button.

2. Add celery, onion, carrot, garlic, tomato paste, thyme, oregano, peppercorns, and water to pot and stir well. Close lid, set steam release to Sealing, press the Manual button, and set time to 60 minutes.

3. When the timer beeps, let pressure release naturally, about 30 minutes. Open lid. Carefully lift out beef and reserve for another use. Strain broth into a jar and use immediately, refrigerate for up to seven days, or freeze for up to three months.

PER SERVING

CALORIES: 27 | FAT: 2g | PROTEIN: 2g | SODIUM: 217mg
FIBER: 0g | CARBOHYDRATES: 1g | SUGAR: 0g

BEEF FOR BROTH

The best cuts of beef for making broth are fattier, tougher cuts that require long cooking, like chuck and round roast. The meat must be cooked long enough for the connective tissue and collagen to break down, giving the broth body and flavor.

Chicken Stock

Save chicken bones from roasted chicken, grilled chicken, rotisserie chicken from the grocery store, soups, or broth in order to make this recipe.

- **Hands-On Time: 5 minutes**
- **Cook Time: 40 minutes**

Serves 8

Cooked chicken bones from 2 (3-pound) chickens
2 stalks celery, chopped
½ cup celery leaves
1 medium yellow onion, peeled and quartered
2 cloves garlic, peeled and crushed
1 bay leaf
2 sprigs fresh thyme
1 teaspoon (about 10) whole black peppercorns
1 sprig fresh sage

1 Place all ingredients in the Instant Pot®, then fill pot with water to the Max Fill line. Close lid, set steam release to Sealing, press the Manual button, and set time to 40 minutes.

2 When the timer beeps, let pressure release naturally, about 30 minutes. Open lid. Strain stock into a jar and use immediately, refrigerate for up to seven days, or freeze for up to three months.

PER SERVING

CALORIES: 14 | FAT: 1g | PROTEIN: 1g | SODIUM: 17mg
FIBER: 0g | CARBOHYDRATES: 1g | SUGAR: 0g

Turkey Stock

Stock is the best way to wring out every last bit of flavor from your Thanksgiving turkey.

- **Hands-On Time: 5 minutes**
- **Cook Time: 40 minutes**

Serves 8

1 carcass from a 12-pound turkey, broken into pieces
3 stalks celery, chopped
½ cup celery leaves
1 medium yellow onion, peeled and quartered
1 medium carrot, chopped
2 cloves garlic, peeled and crushed
2 bay leaves
10 whole black peppercorns
1 sprig fresh sage

1 Place all ingredients in the Instant Pot®, then fill pot with water to the Max Fill line. Close lid, set steam release to Sealing, press the Manual button, and set time to 40 minutes.

2 When the timer beeps, let pressure release naturally, about 30 minutes. Open lid. Strain stock into a jar and use immediately, refrigerate for up to seven days, or freeze for up to three months.

PER SERVING

CALORIES: 13 | FAT: 0g | PROTEIN: 2g | SODIUM: 7mg
FIBER: 0g | CARBOHYDRATES: 1g | SUGAR: 0g

Beef Stock

The Instant Pot® extracts flavor faster than traditional stove top cooking methods because it raises the cooking temperature above water's boiling point, causing the gelatin and collagen in bones to melt faster. To ensure your bones fit in your pot, ask your butcher to cut them into 3" pieces.

- **Hands-On Time: 15 minutes**
- **Cook Time: 2 hours, plus 1 hour for roasting**

Serves 8

5 pounds beef bones
2 tablespoons olive oil, divided
2 stalks celery, chopped
1 medium white onion, peeled and quartered
1 medium carrot, peeled and cut into 2" pieces
½ cup water
2 cloves garlic, peeled and crushed
2 sprigs fresh thyme or ½ teaspoon dried thyme
1 sprig fresh flat-leaf parsley
1 tablespoon tomato paste

BROTH OR STOCK?

Broth is made primarily from meat, and it's simmered with vegetables and herbs to add flavor. Broth is thinner, faster to prepare, and has a lot of flavor. Stock, on the other hand, is made mostly from bones, along with vegetables and herbs. The bones release collagen into the cooking liquid. The collagen in stock adds a rich texture to recipes but not as much flavor.

1. Heat oven to 400°F. Toss beef bones in 1 tablespoon oil and arrange on a large rimmed baking sheet. In a large bowl, toss celery, onion, and carrot with remaining 1 tablespoon oil and set aside.

2. Roast bones for 30 minutes. Remove baking sheet from oven, turn bones over, and add vegetable mixture to the baking sheet. Return baking sheet to oven and roast 30 minutes more until bones are browned and vegetables are soft. Watch bones carefully to avoid scorching.

3. Transfer bones and vegetables to the Instant Pot®. Pour water onto baking sheet and scrape up browned bits. Pour into pot.

4. Add garlic, thyme, parsley, and tomato paste to pot, then cover with water to the Max Fill line. Close lid, set steam release to Sealing, press the Manual button, and set time to 2 hours.

5. When the timer beeps, let pressure release naturally, about 30 minutes. Open lid. Strain stock into a jar and use immediately, refrigerate for up to seven days, or freeze for up to three months.

PER SERVING

CALORIES: 31 | FAT: 2g | PROTEIN: 2g | SODIUM: 22mg
FIBER: 0g | CARBOHYDRATES: 1g | SUGAR: 0g

Vegetable Broth

Vegetable Broth offers a rich, hearty flavor and is perfect for soups when you are looking to substitute meat-based broths. The nutritional yeast called for in this recipe adds an extra savory note to the broth, but if you are unable to find it you can leave it out. This broth is also a great place to use up vegetable scraps, so toss in what you have. It will only make the broth taste better!

- **Hands-On Time: 10 minutes**
- **Cook Time: 30 minutes**

Serves 8

1 tablespoon olive oil
1 medium yellow onion, unpeeled and chopped
4 stalks celery, chopped
4 medium carrots, unpeeled and chopped
2 cups sliced mushrooms
2 medium tomatoes, chopped
6 cloves garlic, peeled and smashed
3 sprigs fresh thyme
3 sprigs fresh tarragon
3 sprigs fresh parsley
2 bay leaves
1 tablespoon nutritional yeast

1 Press the Sauté button on the Instant Pot® and heat oil. Add onion, celery, and carrots. Cook, stirring often, for 5 minutes, then add mushrooms, tomatoes, and garlic and cook for 3 minutes more, or until all the vegetables are tender and the garlic is fragrant. Press the Cancel button.

2 Add thyme, tarragon, parsley, bay leaves, and nutritional yeast to pot, then fill pot with water to the Max Fill line. Close lid, set steam release to Sealing, press the Manual button, and set time to 30 minutes.

3 When the timer beeps, let pressure release naturally, about 30 minutes. Open lid. Strain broth into a jar and use immediately, refrigerate for up to seven days, or freeze for up to three months.

PER SERVING

CALORIES: 20 | FAT: 2g | PROTEIN: 0g | SODIUM: 4mg
FIBER: 0g | CARBOHYDRATES: 1g | SUGAR: 0g

Roasted Vegetable Stock

Roasting vegetables before using them for stock gives them a sweeter, earthier flavor. You can reduce the oven temperature to 375°F if needed after 30 minutes if you feel they are browning too quickly. You want them well roasted, so allow them to brown well but not burn.

- **Hands-On Time: 10 minutes**
- **Cook Time: 30 minutes, plus 1 hour for roasting**

Serves 8

8 stalks celery, cut in half

4 medium sweet onions, peeled and quartered

4 medium carrots, cut in half

4 Roma tomatoes, cut in half

1 fennel bulb, quartered

1 medium green bell pepper, seeded and quartered

4 cloves garlic, peeled and crushed

2 tablespoons olive oil

5 sprigs fresh parsley

5 sprigs fresh tarragon

2 bay leaves

POT BROWNING

You can brown the vegetables for this stock in the Instant Pot® instead of in the oven. Press the Sauté button and heat 1 tablespoon oil. Brown the vegetables for 20–30 minutes, turning often, in 3–4 batches, adding more oil as needed. Skip browning tomatoes this way because they will likely disintegrate while cooking.

1 Heat oven to 400°F. Place celery, onions, carrots, tomatoes, fennel, bell pepper, and garlic on a large rimmed baking sheet. Drizzle with oil and toss to coat.

2 Roast for 1 hour, turning vegetables every 10 minutes to avoid burning. If vegetables start to blacken, remove them from the baking sheet.

3 Add roasted vegetables, parsley, tarragon, and bay leaves to the Instant Pot®, then fill pot with water to the Max Fill line. Close lid, set steam release to Sealing, press the Manual button, and set time to 30 minutes.

4 When the timer beeps, let pressure release naturally, about 30 minutes. Open lid. Strain stock into a jar and use immediately, refrigerate for up to seven days, or freeze for up to three months.

PER SERVING

CALORIES: 20 | FAT: 2g | PROTEIN: 0g | SODIUM: 6mg
FIBER: 0g | CARBOHYDRATES: 1g | SUGAR: 1g

Ham Stock

Don't toss the bones from your spiral-sliced or baked holiday hams. They are packed with flavor and are perfect for making a savory ham stock.

- **Hands-On Time: 5 minutes**
- **Cook Time: 1 hour**

Serves 8

1 cooked ham bone (about 2 pounds)
2 stalks celery, chopped
1 medium yellow onion, peeled and quartered
1 medium carrot, peeled and chopped
2 cloves garlic, peeled and crushed
5 sprigs fresh cilantro
2 bay leaves

1 Place all ingredients in the Instant Pot®, then fill pot with water to the Max Fill line. Close lid, set steam release to Sealing, press the Manual button, and set time to 60 minutes.

2 When the timer beeps, let pressure release naturally, about 30 minutes. Open lid. Strain stock into a jar and use immediately, refrigerate for up to seven days, or freeze for up to three months.

PER SERVING

CALORIES: 21 | FAT: 2g | PROTEIN: 1g | SODIUM: 111mg
FIBER: 0g | CARBOHYDRATES: 0g | SUGAR: 0g

Pork Stock

The easiest way to make this stock is to save the bones from pork roasts and pork chops.

- **Hands-On Time: 5 minutes**
- **Cook Time: 1 hour, 30 minutes**

Serves 8

4 pounds cooked pork bones
2 stalks celery, chopped
1 medium white onion, peeled and quartered
1 medium carrot, peeled and chopped
2 cloves garlic, peeled and crushed
2 sprigs fresh thyme
1 sprig fresh sage

1 Place all ingredients in the Instant Pot®, then add water to the Max Fill line. Close lid, set steam release to Sealing, press the Manual button, and set time to 90 minutes.

2 When the timer beeps, let pressure release naturally, about 30 minutes. Open lid. Strain stock into a jar and use immediately, refrigerate for up to seven days, or freeze for up to three months.

PER SERVING

CALORIES: 17 | FAT: 1g | PROTEIN: 1g | SODIUM: 3mg
FIBER: 0g | CARBOHYDRATES: 0g | SUGAR: 0g

Fish Stock

Fish stock is milder than shellfish-based stocks, and it can be used as the base of fish stews, soups, and chowders.

- **Hands-On Time: 5 minutes**
- **Cook Time: 30 minutes**

Serves 8

1 pound fish bones and heads
1 medium yellow onion, peeled and chopped
2 stalks celery, chopped
1 large carrot, peeled and chopped
3 cloves garlic, peeled and smashed
1 bay leaf
10 whole black peppercorns
½ teaspoon salt
¼ cup white wine

1 Place all ingredients in the Instant Pot®, then fill pot with water to the Max Fill line. Close lid, set steam release to Sealing, press the Manual button, and set time to 30 minutes.

2 When the timer beeps, let pressure release naturally, about 30 minutes. Open lid. Strain stock into a jar and use immediately, refrigerate for up to three days, or freeze for up to three months.

PER SERVING

CALORIES: 13 | FAT: 0g | PROTEIN: 2g | SODIUM: 146mg
FIBER: 0g | CARBOHYDRATES: 0g | SUGAR: 0g

Seafood Stock

While this recipe calls for shrimp shells, you can use any seafood shells you like. Lobster, crab, and crawfish shells can be used to give this stock amazing flavor.

- **Hands-On Time: 5 minutes**
- **Cook Time: 30 minutes**

Serves 8

1 pound shrimp shells and heads
1 medium yellow onion, peeled and chopped
2 stalks celery, chopped
1 large carrot, peeled and chopped
3 cloves garlic, peeled and smashed
2 bay leaves
1 teaspoon seafood seasoning
½ teaspoon salt

1 Place all ingredients in the Instant Pot®, then fill pot with water to the Max Fill line. Close lid, set steam release to Sealing, press the Manual button, and set time to 30 minutes.

2 When the timer beeps, let pressure release naturally, about 30 minutes. Open lid. Strain stock into a jar and use immediately, refrigerate for up to three days, or freeze for up to three months.

PER SERVING

CALORIES: 11 | FAT: 0g | PROTEIN: 2g | SODIUM: 159mg
FIBER: 0g | CARBOHYDRATES: 0g | SUGAR: 0g

Bone Broth

Bone broth varies from stock in the amount of cooking time and gelatin extracted from the bones. Bone broth reportedly helps with joint health, skin health, and hair condition because of the glucosamine and collagen content. Traditionally made bone broth can take as many as 24 hours of simmering, but in the Instant Pot® it takes just a few hours. Bone broth can also be made with chicken or pork bones, or a mixture of beef, chicken, and pork.

- **Hands-On Time: 5 minutes**
- **Cook Time: 2 hours**

Serves 8

3 pounds beef bones

2 stalks celery, cut into 2" pieces

1 medium yellow onion, unpeeled and quartered

1 medium carrot, unpeeled and cut into 2" pieces

2 cloves garlic, unpeeled and crushed

2 sprigs fresh thyme

2 sprigs fresh parsley

1 bay leaf

1 tablespoon apple cider vinegar

1 teaspoon (about 10) whole black peppercorns

THE BENEFITS OF BONE BROTH

Enjoy bone broth alone as a snack or add it to stews, soups, and gravies for improved texture and flavor.

1. Place all ingredients in the Instant Pot®, then fill pot with water to the Max Fill line. Close lid, set steam release to Sealing, press the Manual button, adjust pressure to Low, and set time to 120 minutes.

2. When the timer beeps, let pressure release naturally, about 30 minutes. Open lid. Strain broth into a jar and use immediately, refrigerate for up to seven days, or freeze for up to three months.

PER SERVING

CALORIES: 49 | FAT: 2g | PROTEIN: 8g | SODIUM: 19mg
FIBER: 0g | CARBOHYDRATES: 0g | SUGAR: 0g

Consommé

Consommé is a clarified soup made from bone-in chicken and vegetables. The cooked vegetables and chicken are made into a paste with egg whites and added back to the pot.

- **Hands-On Time: 45 minutes**
- **Cook Time: 42 minutes**

Serves 8

3 pounds bone-in, skinless chicken pieces

2 stalks celery, cut into 4" pieces

2 medium yellow onions, peeled and cut in half

2 medium carrots, peeled and cut into 2" pieces

6 button mushrooms, cut in half

2 cloves garlic, unpeeled and crushed

3 sprigs fresh thyme

3 sprigs fresh parsley

1 bay leaf

1 tablespoon apple cider vinegar

1 teaspoon (about 10) whole black peppercorns

1 teaspoon coriander seeds

6 cups Chicken Stock (see recipe in this chapter)

4 cups water

4 egg whites

½ teaspoon salt

1 tablespoon dry sherry

1 Place chicken, celery, onions, carrots, mushrooms, garlic, thyme, parsley, bay leaf, vinegar, peppercorns, coriander seeds, stock, and water in the Instant Pot®. Close lid, set steam release to Sealing, press the Manual button, and set time to 40 minutes.

2 When the timer beeps, allow pressure to release naturally, about 30 minutes. Press the Cancel button, open lid, and discard bay leaf. Strain stock through a fine-mesh sieve with three layers of cheesecloth into a large bowl. Transfer strained liquid back to pot.

3 Allow solids to cool for 10 minutes. Remove chicken from bones. Transfer chicken and vegetables to a food processor. Pulse ten times, then add egg whites and pulse until a rough paste is formed. Add paste to pot.

4 Close lid, set steam release to Sealing, press the Manual button, adjust pressure to Low, and adjust time to 2 minutes. When the timer beeps, quick-release the pressure and remove lid. The solids will form a layer on top of stock.

5 Press the Cancel button, then press the Sauté button. Carefully break a hole in the solids layer and ladle stock over the solids every few minutes for 30 minutes.

6 Carefully ladle stock through a strainer lined with cheesecloth into a large clean bowl. Discard solids. Allow stock to cool and strain off any fat. Season with salt and sherry.

PER SERVING

CALORIES: 11 | FAT: 0g | PROTEIN: 1g | SODIUM: 174mg
FIBER: 0g | CARBOHYDRATES: 1g | SUGAR: 0g

Mushroom Stock

Dried mushrooms have a concentrated flavor that adds rich umami flavor to this vegan stock. They are available at most grocery stores in small bags or in the bulk section of some health food stores.

- **Hands-On Time: 10 minutes**
- **Cook Time: 30 minutes**

Serves 8

1 tablespoon olive oil

1 medium yellow onion, unpeeled and chopped

2 stalks celery, chopped

4 cups sliced mushrooms

1 medium carrot, unpeeled and chopped

4 ounces dried mixed mushrooms

3 cloves garlic, peeled and smashed

2 sprigs fresh thyme

2 bay leaves

1 tablespoon nutritional yeast

THE MAGIC OF MUSHROOMS
Mushrooms have a long culinary history dating back to around A.D. 600 in Asia when they were first grown or foraged for cooking purposes. Today, mushrooms are a popular addition to the modern diet—especially the button mushroom, which accounts for almost 40 percent of the mushrooms grown today.

1 Press the Sauté button on the Instant Pot® and heat oil. Add onion, celery, sliced mushrooms, and carrot. Cook, stirring often, for 5 minutes. Press the Cancel button.

2 Add dried mushrooms, garlic, thyme, bay leaves, and nutritional yeast to pot, then fill pot with water to the Max Fill line. Close lid, set steam release to Sealing, press the Manual button, and set time to 30 minutes.

3 When the timer beeps, let pressure release naturally, about 30 minutes. Open lid. Strain stock into a jar and use immediately, refrigerate for up to seven days, or freeze for up to three months.

PER SERVING

CALORIES: 22 | FAT: 2g | PROTEIN: 1g | SODIUM: 2mg
FIBER: 0g | CARBOHYDRATES: 2g | SUGAR: 0g

Classic Soups

If you think of traditional comfort food soups, what comes to mind? If you are like most people, you are likely to think of classics like rich chicken noodle soup, creamy broccoli cheese soup, or perhaps hearty tortilla soup. These soups are popular for good reason. They have warm, familiar flavors that everyone loves.

The Instant Pot® makes a warm bowl of classic comfort no more than minutes away. Forget stirring and standing over a hot stove, waiting for your soup to finally be done. The Instant Pot® leaves you free to spend time with friends and family while a delicious meal cooks in record time. Classic soups are wonderful candidates for weekly meal prep. A little time spent chopping and measuring on the weekend means that weeknight meals can often be as easy as dump, set, and enjoy. Leftovers also make a tasty lunch that will have coworkers and schoolmates envious!

You will find all the classics here—from Vegetable Barley Soup to Loaded Baked Potato Soup, and even Vegan Broccoli "Cheese" Soup. With the Instant Pot® in your kitchen you are never far from the classic soups you love!

French Onion Soup

Caramelized onions, hearty Beef Stock, and broiled cheese combine to make a deeply savory soup that is perfect as the first course of a dinner party.

- **Hands-On Time: 35 minutes**
- **Cook Time: 45 minutes**

Serves 8

6 tablespoons salted butter, divided

3 pounds sweet onions, peeled and sliced

1 tablespoon light brown sugar

¼ cup white wine

2 cloves garlic, peeled and smashed

1 tablespoon balsamic vinegar

1 bay leaf

½ teaspoon dried thyme

¼ teaspoon ground black pepper

4 cups Beef Stock (see recipe in Chapter 2)

4 cups Beef Broth (see recipe in Chapter 2)

8 (1"-thick) slices French baguette

1 cup grated Gruyère cheese

1 Press the Sauté button on the Instant Pot® and melt 3 tablespoons butter. Add onions and brown sugar. Cook until onions are just tender, about 5 minutes. Press the Cancel button. Close lid, set steam release to Sealing, press the Manual button, and adjust time to 15 minutes. When the timer beeps, quick-release the pressure and press the Cancel button.

2 Drain off the excess liquid from pot. Return pot to machine and press the Sauté button. Add remaining butter, and cook, stirring frequently, until onions are caramelized and brown, about 15–20 minutes.

3 Add wine to pot and scrape up any browned bits from pot. Press the Cancel button. Add garlic, vinegar, bay leaf, thyme, pepper, stock, and broth to pot. Close lid, set steam release to Sealing, press the Manual button, and set time to 20 minutes. When the timer beeps, let pressure release naturally, about 20 minutes. Press the Cancel button, open lid, and stir well. Remove and discard bay leaf.

4 Press the Sauté button and simmer soup for 10 minutes, stirring often, to thicken. While soup simmers, heat oven broiler.

5 Divide soup into heatproof soup bowls. Place a slice of bread on each bowl, then divide cheese over bowls. Broil for 3–5 minutes, or until cheese is bubbling and brown. Serve hot.

PER SERVING

CALORIES: 277 | FAT: 11g | PROTEIN: 11g | SODIUM: 394mg
FIBER: 3g | CARBOHYDRATES: 33g | SUGAR: 10g

Chicken Noodle Soup

This from-scratch soup is ready in about an hour from start to finish, thanks to the Instant Pot®. If you have homemade Chicken Broth (see recipe in Chapter 2) on hand, you can use it here to supercharge the flavor. For a gluten-free version, use your favorite gluten-free noodles, or eliminate them altogether.

- **Hands-On Time: 15 minutes**
- **Cook Time: 24 minutes**

Serves 8

1 (3½-pound) chicken, cut into pieces

3 stalks celery, chopped

2 medium carrots, peeled and chopped

1 medium yellow onion, peeled and chopped

1 clove garlic, peeled and smashed

1 bay leaf

1 teaspoon poultry seasoning

½ teaspoon dried thyme

1 teaspoon salt

¼ teaspoon ground black pepper

4 cups low-sodium chicken broth

4 ounces dried egg noodles

1 Place chicken, celery, carrots, onion, garlic, bay leaf, poultry seasoning, thyme, salt, pepper, and broth in the Instant Pot®. Close lid, set steam release to Sealing, press the Soup button, and cook for the default time of 20 minutes.

2 When the timer beeps, let pressure release naturally, about 20–25 minutes. Press the Cancel button and open lid.

3 Remove and discard bay leaf. With tongs or a slotted spoon, transfer chicken to a cutting board. Carefully shred chicken, discarding skin and bones. Return chicken to pot and stir to combine. Add noodles, close lid, set steam release to Sealing, press the Manual button, and set time to 4 minutes.

4 When the timer beeps, quick-release the pressure, remove lid, and stir well. Serve hot.

PER SERVING

CALORIES: 219 | FAT: 8g | PROTEIN: 19g | SODIUM: 420mg
FIBER: 2g | CARBOHYDRATES: 16g | SUGAR: 2g

Vegetable Beef Soup

Less expensive cuts of beef, such as chuck roast, are best for this recipe as they add a deep, fatty flavor and are incredibly tender once cooked. The Instant Pot® cuts the cooking time of this traditionally long-cooked soup, so when you are in need of a bowl of filling beefy soup you can have it in about an hour! Beef broth adds the most flavor to this soup, but substituting ¼ of the broth for stock or bone broth will add a richer texture.

- **Hands-On Time: 25 minutes**
- **Cook Time: 20 minutes**

Serves 8

2 pounds boneless chuck roast, cut into 1" pieces

¼ cup all-purpose flour

1 teaspoon salt, divided

1 teaspoon ground black pepper, divided

2 tablespoons vegetable oil, divided

2 medium yellow onions, peeled and chopped

2 medium carrots, peeled and chopped

2 stalks celery, chopped

2 cloves garlic, peeled and minced

¼ teaspoon dried thyme

1 russet potato, peeled and cut into ½" cubes

1 (14-ounce) can diced tomatoes, undrained

4 cups Vegetable Broth (see recipe in Chapter 2)

2 cups water

1 Place beef, flour, and ½ teaspoon each salt and pepper in a large zip-top plastic bag. Shake well, making sure beef is evenly coated.

2 Press the Sauté button on the Instant Pot® and heat 1 tablespoon oil. Add half of beef to pot, making sure there is a little space between each piece. Brown for 2–3 minutes per side. Transfer beef to a plate and repeat with remaining oil and beef.

3 Add onions, carrots, and celery to pot. Cook until just tender, about 5 minutes. Add garlic and thyme and cook until fragrant, about 30 seconds. Press the Cancel button.

4 Return beef to pot. Add potato, tomatoes, broth, and water. Stir well, making sure to scrape up any bits on the bottom of pot. Close lid, set steam release to Sealing, press the Soup button, and cook for the default time of 20 minutes.

5 When the timer beeps, let pressure release naturally, about 15 minutes. Open lid and stir in remaining ½ teaspoon each salt and pepper. Serve hot.

PER SERVING

CALORIES: 312 | FAT: 17g | PROTEIN: 24g | SODIUM: 495mg
FIBER: 2g | CARBOHYDRATES: 16g | SUGAR: 3g

Italian Wedding Soup

Italian Wedding Soup is the perfect marriage of vegetables, greens, and meatballs. The soup makes a filling meal, and leftovers are wonderful for lunch. If making the meatballs seems too daunting, or if you want to save even more time, you can use ½ pound of sliced Italian sausage in its place. You can bulk this soup up even more by adding a can of drained and rinsed cannellini beans.

- **Hands-On Time: 30 minutes**
- **Cook Time: 25 minutes**

Serves 8

½ medium yellow onion, peeled and minced

1 large egg, beaten

1 clove garlic, peeled and minced

¼ cup bread crumbs

½ teaspoon Italian seasoning

1 teaspoon salt, divided

¼ teaspoon crushed red pepper flakes

8 ounces ground pork

4 ounces 90% lean ground beef

1 tablespoon vegetable oil

1 medium yellow onion, peeled and roughly chopped

1 medium carrot, peeled and chopped

1 stalk celery, chopped

2 cloves garlic, chopped

½ teaspoon dried thyme

½ teaspoon ground black pepper

⅓ cup white wine

4 cups Vegetable Broth (see recipe in Chapter 2)

2 cups water

8 ounces baby spinach

1. In a large bowl combine minced onion, egg, minced garlic, bread crumbs, Italian seasoning, ½ teaspoon salt, red pepper flakes, ground pork, and ground beef. Gently mix until well combined. Roll into ½" meatballs. Place on a tray and refrigerate until ready to cook.

2. Press the Sauté button on the Instant Pot® and heat oil. Add onion, carrot, and celery and cook until just tender, about 5 minutes. Add chopped garlic, thyme, and pepper. Cook for 30 seconds. Add wine, scraping the bottom of pot, and cook for 30 seconds. Press the Cancel button.

3. Add Vegetable Broth, water, and remaining ½ teaspoon salt. Carefully drop in the meatballs. Close lid, set steam release to Sealing, press the Soup button, and cook for the default time of 20 minutes.

4. When the timer beeps, let pressure release naturally, about 15 minutes. Open lid and stir in spinach. Replace the lid, press the Keep Warm button, and simmer for 5 minutes. Serve hot.

PER SERVING

CALORIES: 158 | FAT: 9g | PROTEIN: 10g | SODIUM: 387mg
FIBER: 2g | CARBOHYDRATES: 8g | SUGAR: 2g

Pasta e Fagioli

The name of this soup translates to "pasta and beans," but it is so much more elegant than it sounds. The spicy sausage and fresh herbs provide a lively flavor. For a vegetarian version, swap out the Chicken Broth for Vegetable Broth (see recipe in Chapter 2), and the sausage for meatless crumbles cooked with a teaspoon of Italian seasoning and a tablespoon or two of vegetable oil.

- **Hands-On Time: 20 minutes**
- **Cook Time: 23 minutes**

Serves 8

1 pound bulk Italian sausage

1 medium yellow onion, peeled and chopped

2 stalks celery, chopped

1 large carrot, peeled and chopped

2 cloves garlic, peeled and chopped

½ teaspoon dried thyme

1 teaspoon Italian seasoning

½ teaspoon ground black pepper

1 (15-ounce) can diced tomatoes, undrained

4 cups Chicken Broth (see recipe in Chapter 2)

1 cup water

1 cup dried cannellini beans, soaked overnight and drained

1 cup ditalini pasta

1 cup grated Parmesan cheese

2 tablespoons chopped fresh flat-leaf parsley

2 tablespoons chopped fresh basil

1 Press the Sauté button on the Instant Pot®. Add sausage and cook, crumbling into bite-sized pieces, until browned, about 8 minutes. Add onion, celery, and carrot and cook until just tender, about 5 minutes. Add garlic, thyme, Italian seasoning, and pepper. Cook for 30 seconds. Add tomatoes, scraping the bottom of pot, and cook for 30 seconds. Press the Cancel button.

2 Add broth, water, and beans. Stir well. Close lid, set steam release to Sealing, press the Soup button, and cook for the default time of 20 minutes.

3 When the timer beeps, let pressure release naturally, about 15 minutes. Open lid and stir in pasta. Press the Cancel button, close lid, set steam release to Sealing, press the Manual button, and set time to 3 minutes. When the timer beeps, quick-release the pressure. Open lid and stir well.

4 Divide soup into bowls. Top each with cheese, parsley, and basil. Serve hot.

PER SERVING

CALORIES: 449 | FAT: 21g | PROTEIN: 23g | SODIUM: 760mg
FIBER: 7g | CARBOHYDRATES: 41g | SUGAR: 3g

Broccoli Cheese Soup

If you like a few larger chunks of broccoli, you can strain some out before blending, then stir them back in. The Gruyère in this soup is robust and nutty, and adds a sophisticated flavor when blended with the Cheddar. If you are unable to find Gruyère cheese, you can substitute Swiss or sharp Cheddar for a tangier flavor.

- **Hands-On Time: 20 minutes**
- **Cook Time: 5 minutes**

Serves 8

3 tablespoons unsalted butter

2 medium carrots, peeled and finely chopped

2 stalks celery, finely chopped

1 medium yellow onion, peeled and finely chopped

1 clove garlic, peeled and minced

½ teaspoon dried thyme

3 cups chopped broccoli florets, divided

¼ cup all-purpose flour

3 cups Chicken Broth (see recipe in Chapter 2)

1 tablespoon water

½ cup heavy cream

2 cups shredded mild Cheddar cheese

1 cup shredded Gruyère cheese

1 Press the Sauté button on the Instant Pot® and melt butter. Add carrots, celery, and onion. Cook, stirring often, until softened, about 5 minutes. Add garlic and cook until fragrant, about 30 seconds, then add thyme and 2 cups broccoli and stir well.

2 Add flour and stir well to combine, then cook for 1 minute. Slowly stir in broth, scraping the bottom of pot well. Press the Cancel button.

3 Close lid, set steam release to Sealing, press the Manual button, and set time to 5 minutes. When the timer beeps, let pressure release naturally, about 15 minutes. Open lid and purée soup with an immersion blender.

4 Place remaining 1 cup broccoli in a medium microwave-safe bowl with water. Cover and microwave for 4 minutes until broccoli is tender. Drain, then add broccoli to pot.

5 Stir in cream, then add cheeses 1 cup at a time, whisking each addition until completely melted before adding another. Serve hot.

PER SERVING

CALORIES: 300 | FAT: 22g | PROTEIN: 13g | SODIUM: 317mg
FIBER: 2g | CARBOHYDRATES: 9g | SUGAR: 2g

Vegan Broccoli "Cheese" Soup

Cashews and nutritional yeast give this soup a creamy, cheesy flavor and texture. You can eat this soup as it is, with crusty bread for dunking, or serve it over baked potatoes or fluffy cooked rice.

- **Hands-On Time: 10 minutes**
- **Cook Time: 6 minutes**

Serves 8

3 tablespoons vegetable oil

3 medium carrots, peeled and finely chopped

1 stalk celery, chopped

1 medium yellow onion, peeled and diced

1 medium russet potato, peeled and chopped

2 cloves garlic, peeled and minced

½ teaspoon dried thyme

¼ teaspoon smoked paprika

½ cup nutritional yeast

½ cup whole raw cashews

4 cups Vegetable Broth (see recipe in Chapter 2)

1 tablespoon lemon juice

3 cups chopped broccoli

½ teaspoon salt

1 Press the Sauté button on the Instant Pot® and heat oil. Add carrots, celery, and onion. Cook, stirring often, until softened, about 5 minutes.

2 Add potato, garlic, thyme, and paprika, and cook until garlic and spices are fragrant, about 30 seconds. Press the Cancel button. Add nutritional yeast, cashews, broth, and lemon juice. Mix well.

3 Close lid, set steam release to Sealing, press the Manual button, and set time to 5 minutes. When the timer beeps, let pressure release naturally, about 15 minutes. Open lid and purée mixture with an immersion blender or in batches in a blender.

4 Add broccoli to pot and stir well. Press the Cancel button, close lid, set steam release to Sealing, press the Manual button, and set time to 1. When the timer beeps, quick-release the pressure. Remove lid, add salt, and stir well. Serve hot.

PER SERVING

CALORIES: 174 | FAT: 10g | PROTEIN: 6g | SODIUM: 187mg
FIBER: 3g | CARBOHYDRATES: 16g | SUGAR: 3g

NUTRITIONAL YEAST

Nutritional yeast is a plant-based seasoning that has a cheesy flavor and aroma. Made from the same strains of yeast used in bread and beer making, nutritional yeast is grown using a sugar-rich base, then deactivated with heat, pasteurized, dried, and crumbled.

Vegetable Barley Soup

Barley is a heart-healthy cereal grain that is full of good-for-you nutrients like potassium, niacin, vitamin B$_6$, and folate. It has lots of fiber, which has been shown to lower cholesterol. This soup is also packed with vegetables, so enjoy as much as you want! It is good tasting and good for you!

- **Hands-On Time: 10 minutes**
- **Cook Time: 30 minutes**

Serves 8

2 tablespoons vegetable oil

½ medium yellow onion, peeled and chopped

1 medium carrot, peeled and chopped

1 stalk celery, chopped

2 cups sliced mushrooms

2 cloves garlic, peeled and minced

½ teaspoon dried thyme

½ teaspoon ground black pepper

1 large russet potato, peeled and cut into ½" cubes

1 (14-ounce) can fire-roasted diced tomatoes, undrained

½ cup medium pearled barley

4 cups Vegetable Broth (see recipe in Chapter 2)

2 cups water

1 (15-ounce) can corn, drained

1 (15-ounce) can cut green beans, drained

1 (15-ounce) can Great Northern beans, drained and rinsed

½ teaspoon salt

1. Press the Sauté button on the Instant Pot® and heat oil. Add onion, carrot, celery, and mushrooms. Cook until just tender, about 5 minutes. Add garlic, thyme, and pepper. Cook for 30 seconds. Press the Cancel button.

2. Add potato, tomatoes, barley, broth, and water. Close lid, set steam release to Sealing, press the Soup button, and cook for the default time of 20 minutes.

3. When the timer beeps, let pressure release naturally, about 15 minutes. Open lid, stir soup, then add corn, green beans, and Great Northern beans. Replace the lid, press the Keep Warm button, and let stand for 10 minutes. Open lid and season with salt. Serve hot.

PER SERVING

CALORIES: 242 | FAT: 5g | PROTEIN: 9g | SODIUM: 512mg
FIBER: 8g | CARBOHYDRATES: 42g | SUGAR: 5g

Beef and Barley Soup

This soup is hearty, full of healthy vegetables, and affordable since it is made with ground beef. If you have it, use leftover beef, such as roast beef, steak, or stew meat, instead of ground beef. You'll save a few minutes since you will not need to brown it. Warm bread or biscuits with butter are the perfect accompaniment to this soup.

- Hands-On Time: 20 minutes
- Cook Time: 25 minutes

Serves 8

1 tablespoon vegetable oil

½ pound 90% lean ground beef

½ medium yellow onion, peeled and chopped

1 medium carrot, peeled and chopped

1 stalk celery, chopped

1 medium green bell pepper, seeded and chopped

1 (15-ounce) can diced tomatoes, undrained

1 large russet potato, peeled and cut into ½" cubes

½ cup medium pearled barley

2 cloves garlic, peeled and minced

½ teaspoon dried thyme

½ teaspoon ground black pepper

4 cups Beef Broth (see recipe in Chapter 2)

2 cups water

1 (15-ounce) can cut green beans, drained

½ teaspoon salt

1 Press the Sauté button on the Instant Pot® and heat oil. Add beef and brown well, about 8 minutes. Add onion, carrot, celery, and bell pepper. Cook until just tender, about 5 minutes. Add tomatoes, potato, barley, garlic, thyme, black pepper, broth, and water. Press the Cancel button.

2 Close lid, set steam release to Sealing, press the Soup button, and cook for the default time of 20 minutes. When the timer beeps, let pressure release naturally, about 15 minutes. Open lid, stir soup, and add green beans and salt. Replace the lid, press the Keep Warm button, and simmer for 5 minutes. Serve hot.

PER SERVING

CALORIES: 190 | FAT: 5g | PROTEIN: 10g | SODIUM: 450mg
FIBER: 5g | CARBOHYDRATES: 25g | SUGAR: 3g

Beef Noodle Soup

While searing and browning the beef may take a little bit of time, it is worth it for the ultimate reward when the soup is ready. Browning makes the beef look more appealing, and it adds a caramelized flavor to this rustic soup.

- **Hands-On Time: 30 minutes**
- **Cook Time: 24 minutes**

Serves 8

2 pounds boneless chuck roast, cut into 1" pieces

¼ cup all-purpose flour

1 teaspoon salt, divided

1 teaspoon ground black pepper, divided

2 tablespoons vegetable oil, divided

2 medium yellow onions, peeled and chopped

2 medium carrots, peeled and chopped

2 stalks celery, chopped

2 cloves garlic, peeled and minced

1 tablespoon tomato paste

¼ teaspoon dried thyme

1 (14-ounce) can diced tomatoes, undrained

4 cups Beef Broth (see recipe in Chapter 2)

2 cups water

4 ounces elbow macaroni

1 Place beef, flour, and ½ teaspoon each salt and pepper in a large zip-top plastic bag. Shake well, making sure beef is evenly coated.

2 Press the Sauté button on the Instant Pot® and heat 1 tablespoon oil. Add half of the beef to pot, making sure there is a little space between each piece. Brown for 2–3 minutes per side. Transfer beef to a plate and repeat with remaining oil and beef.

3 Add onions, carrots, and celery to pot. Cook until just tender, about 5 minutes. Add garlic, tomato paste, and thyme and cook until fragrant, about 1 minute. Press the Cancel button.

4 Return beef to pot. Add tomatoes, broth, and water. Stir well, making sure to scrape up any bits on the bottom of pot. Close lid, set steam release to Sealing, press the Soup button, and cook for the default time of 20 minutes.

5 When the timer beeps, let pressure release naturally, about 15 minutes. Open lid and stir in remaining ½ teaspoon each salt and pepper. Press the Cancel button.

6 Add macaroni to pot and stir well. Close lid, set steam release to Sealing, press the Manual button, and set time to 4 minutes. When the timer beeps, quick-release the pressure. Open lid and stir well. Serve hot.

PER SERVING

CALORIES: 355 | **FAT:** 18g | **PROTEIN:** 26g | **SODIUM:** 616mg
FIBER: 3g | **CARBOHYDRATES:** 22g | **SUGAR:** 4g

Creamy Chicken and Rice Soup

If you have leftover cooked rice or a bag of ready-cooked rice from the grocery store, you can use that here. Use 1 cup of ready-cooked rice, and instead of cooking again for 4 minutes, just let the soup stand on the Keep Warm setting for 10–15 minutes.

- Hands-On Time: 20 minutes
- Cook Time: 24 minutes

Serves 8

3 tablespoons unsalted butter

3 stalks celery, chopped

2 medium carrots, peeled and chopped

1 medium yellow onion, peeled and chopped

2 cloves garlic, peeled and smashed

2 tablespoons all-purpose flour

4 cups Chicken Broth, divided (see recipe in Chapter 2)

1 bay leaf

1 teaspoon poultry seasoning

½ teaspoon dried thyme

1 teaspoon salt

¼ teaspoon ground black pepper

1 (3-pound) chicken, cut into pieces

½ cup uncooked white rice

½ cup heavy whipping cream

1 Press the Sauté button on the Instant Pot® and melt butter. Add celery, carrots, and onion. Cook, stirring often, until vegetables soften, about 5 minutes. Add garlic and cook for 30 seconds, then add flour and cook for 1 minute. Stir in 2 cups broth and stir well, making sure to scrape any bits from the bottom of the pot. Press the Cancel button.

2 Add bay leaf, poultry seasoning, thyme, salt, and pepper to pot. Stir well, then add chicken and cover with remaining broth to the Max Fill line. Close lid, set steam release to Sealing, press the Soup button, and cook for the default time of 20 minutes.

3 When the timer beeps, let pressure release naturally, about 20–25 minutes. Press the Cancel button and open lid.

4 Remove and discard bay leaf. With tongs or a slotted spoon transfer chicken to a cutting board. Carefully shred meat, discarding skin and bones. Return chicken to pot and stir to combine. Add rice, close lid, set steam release to Sealing, press the Manual button, and set time to 4 minutes.

5 When the timer beeps, quick-release the pressure, remove lid, and stir well. Add cream and stir. Serve hot.

PER SERVING

CALORIES: 232 | FAT: 13g | PROTEIN: 12g | SODIUM: 355mg
FIBER: 1g | CARBOHYDRATES: 14g | SUGAR: 1g

Tortilla Soup

Tortilla Soup is a great make-ahead soup that only improves with time. Divide leftovers in jars or containers and have them ready for meals all week. The soup can serve as a fun canvas for toppings like diced avocado, lime wedges, sour cream, cilantro leaves, diced tomato and onion, or corn kernels.

- **Hands-On Time: 10 minutes**
- **Cook Time: 15 minutes**

Serves 8

2 tablespoons vegetable oil

1 medium yellow onion, peeled and chopped

2 cloves garlic, peeled and minced

2 jalapeño peppers, seeded and minced

½ teaspoon ground cumin

¼ teaspoon smoked paprika

1 (15-ounce) can fire-roasted tomatoes, undrained

½ cup roughly chopped cilantro

4 cups Chicken Broth (see recipe in Chapter 2) or water

4 cups shredded cooked chicken breast

1 (15-ounce) can pinto beans, drained and rinsed

1 teaspoon salt

¼ teaspoon ground black pepper

¼ cup lime juice

1 cup shredded Cheddar cheese

3 ounces tortilla chips, roughly crushed

1　Press the Sauté button on the Instant Pot® and heat oil. Add onion and cook until tender, about 5 minutes. Add garlic, jalapeños, cumin, and paprika and cook until fragrant, about 1 minute. Press the Cancel button.

2　Stir in tomatoes, cilantro, and broth. Stir well, then close lid, set steam release to Sealing, press the Manual button, and set time to 5 minutes.

3　When the timer beeps, let pressure release naturally for 15 minutes, then quick-release any remaining pressure. Open lid, stir in chicken, beans, salt, pepper, and lime juice. Press the Keep Warm button and let soup stand for 10 minutes.

4　Divide soup among bowls and garnish with cheese and tortilla chips. Serve hot.

PER SERVING

CALORIES: 311 | FAT: 9g | PROTEIN: 31g | SODIUM: 657mg
FIBER: 2g | CARBOHYDRATES: 20g | SUGAR: 2g

Lemony Chicken and Rice Soup

Warm and refreshing, this is a wonderful soup to brighten up a gloomy day! If you want, you can swap rice for pasta. Egg noodles are nice here, and so is orzo, a rice-shaped pasta. The cooking time remains the same when making it with pasta, and it gives the broth a slightly thicker texture.

- **Hands-On Time: 10 minutes**
- **Cook Time: 5 minutes**

Serves 8

2 tablespoons vegetable oil

2 stalks celery, sliced

1 medium carrot, peeled and chopped

1 medium yellow onion, peeled and chopped

2 cloves garlic, peeled and minced

½ teaspoon dried thyme

1 bay leaf

4 cups Chicken Broth (see recipe in Chapter 2) or water

3 cups shredded cooked chicken breast

½ cup uncooked white rice

¼ cup lemon juice

2 tablespoons chopped fresh flat-leaf parsley

1 teaspoon salt

¼ teaspoon ground black pepper

1 Press the Sauté button on the Instant Pot® and heat oil. Add celery, carrot, and onion and cook until tender, about 5 minutes. Add garlic and thyme and cook until fragrant, about 1 minute. Press the Cancel button.

2 Add bay leaf, broth, chicken, and rice. Stir well, then close lid, set steam release to Sealing, press the Manual button, and set time to 5 minutes.

3 When the timer beeps, let pressure release naturally for 15 minutes, then quick-release any remaining pressure. Open lid, stir in lemon juice, parsley, salt, and pepper. Remove and discard bay leaf. Serve hot.

PER SERVING

CALORIES: 194 | FAT: 6g | PROTEIN: 20g | SODIUM: 351mg
FIBER: 1g | CARBOHYDRATES: 13g | SUGAR: 1g

Fresh Tomato Basil Soup

Fresh tomatoes have a delicate, fresh flavor that pairs beautifully with fresh basil. Summer tomatoes are best for this soup, but you can substitute a mix of equal parts hothouse tomatoes and canned whole tomatoes so you can enjoy this soup year-round.

- **Hands-On Time: 20 minutes**
- **Cook Time: 5 minutes**

Serves 4

¼ cup olive oil

1 medium yellow onion, peeled and chopped

4 cloves garlic, minced

8 large tomatoes, peeled and cut into big chunks

1 bay leaf

1 tablespoon sugar

¼ cup chopped basil

1 teaspoon dried oregano

1 teaspoon dried fennel

1 teaspoon salt

½ teaspoon black pepper

2 cups Vegetable Broth or Chicken Broth (see recipes in Chapter 2)

2 tablespoons unsalted butter

½ cup heavy cream

1 Press the Sauté button on the Instant Pot® and heat olive oil. Add onion and cook until soft, about 5 minutes, then add garlic and cook until fragrant, about 30 seconds.

2 Add tomatoes and bay leaf and cook for 4–5 minutes, or until tomatoes start to release their juice.

3 Press the Cancel button and add sugar, basil, oregano, fennel, salt, pepper, and broth. Stir well and close lid. Set steam release to Sealing, press the Manual button, and set time for 5 minutes.

4 When the timer beeps, quick-release the pressure and press the Cancel button. Open lid and stir in butter until melted, then add cream. Discard bay leaf.

5 Purée soup with an immersion blender or transfer to a blender and purée until smooth. If you prefer a slightly chunky soup, only purée half or three-quarters of the soup. Serve hot.

PICKING THE PERFECT TOMATO
When making tomato soup, use paste tomatoes. In your local market, look for firm, plump, bright red Roma tomatoes—the most common paste tomatoes available. If you can find them, San Marzano–style tomatoes are an excellent choice for soups and sauces.

PER SERVING

CALORIES: 378 | **FAT:** 31g | **PROTEIN:** 5g | **SODIUM:** 615mg
FIBER: 5g | **CARBOHYDRATES:** 23g | **SUGAR:** 15g

Tortellini Soup with Kale and Tomato

Fresh tortellini can be found in the refrigerated section in your grocery store's deli, or with the cheeses. You can use whatever filling you like for your pasta, but to keep this recipe vegetarian friendly, cheese is the best option.

- **Hands-On Time: 30 minutes**
- **Cook Time: 5 minutes**

Serves 8

1 tablespoon vegetable oil

1 medium yellow onion, peeled and chopped

2 stalks celery, chopped

1 medium carrot, peeled and chopped

3 cups chopped kale

2 cloves garlic, chopped

1 teaspoon Italian seasoning

½ teaspoon black pepper

1 (15-ounce) can diced tomatoes, drained

4 cups Vegetable Broth (see recipe in Chapter 2)

9 ounces cheese tortellini

½ teaspoon salt

¼ cup chopped fresh flat-leaf parsley

INSTANT POT® PASTA

To cook pasta in the Instant Pot®, add 1 cup water and 1 teaspoon butter or oil for every 4 ounces of pasta. You can also add dried herbs, mustard, salt, or pepper. Close the lid, set the steam release to Sealing, press the Manual button, and cook 4 minutes.

1. Press the Sauté button on the Instant Pot® and heat oil. Add onion, celery, carrot, and kale. Cook until just tender, about 5 minutes. Add garlic, Italian seasoning, and pepper. Cook for 30 seconds. Add tomatoes and cook for 30 seconds. Press the Cancel button.

2. Add broth and 1 cup water. Stir well. Close lid, set steam release to Sealing, press the Manual button, and adjust time to 5 minutes.

3. When the timer beeps, let pressure release naturally, about 15 minutes. Open lid, stir in pasta and salt. Press the Cancel button, close lid, set steam release to Sealing, press the Manual button, and set time to 0. When the timer beeps, quick-release the pressure. Open lid and stir well.

4. Divide soup into bowls. Top each with parsley and serve hot.

PER SERVING

CALORIES: 151 | FAT: 5g | PROTEIN: 5g | SODIUM: 366mg
FIBER: 2g | CARBOHYDRATES: 21g | SUGAR: 3g

Loaded Baked Potato Soup

This soup offers all the best flavors of a baked potato stuffed with cheese, bacon, and sour cream. On top of all that amazing flavor, the Instant Pot® cooks the potatoes to tender perfection, so they're creamy and smooth when you blend them. For extra flavor sauté the onion in a mixture of butter and bacon drippings.

- **Hands-On Time: 15 minutes**
- **Cook Time: 10 minutes**

Serves 8

4 tablespoons unsalted butter

1 medium yellow onion, peeled and chopped

3 tablespoons all-purpose flour

1 teaspoon salt

½ teaspoon ground black pepper

6 cups Chicken Broth (see recipe in Chapter 2)

5 pounds russet potatoes, peeled and cubed

4 ounces cream cheese

1 cup heavy cream

8 slices thick-cut bacon, cooked crisp and chopped

4 scallions, sliced

1 cup shredded Cheddar cheese

1 cup sour cream

1 Press the Sauté button on the Instant Pot® and melt butter. Add onion and cook until tender, about 3 minutes. Add flour, salt, and pepper and cook until flour is moistened, about 1 minute. Slowly whisk in broth, then add potatoes. Press the Cancel button.

2 Close lid, set steam release to Sealing, press the Manual button, and set time to 10 minutes. When the timer beeps, let pressure release naturally, about 15 minutes.

3 Open lid and stir well. With an immersion blender, purée until the soup has some large chunks of potato but is mostly smooth. Add cream cheese and stir until melted, then add cream and stir well. Serve hot with bacon, scallions, Cheddar cheese, and sour cream to garnish.

PER SERVING

CALORIES: 578 | FAT: 40g | PROTEIN: 14g | SODIUM: 657mg
FIBER: 2g | CARBOHYDRATES: 33g | SUGAR: 5g

Split Pea Soup with Ham

Dried split peas are affordable and nutritious, and with the Instant Pot® they take a fraction of the time to prepare. After cooking, you can blend the soup to the consistency you prefer. Blending it at least partway will give it a creamy texture. If you have a leftover ham bone, add it to the pot for even more flavor.

- **Hands-On Time: 10 minutes**
- **Cook Time: 20 minutes**

Serves 8

4 tablespoons unsalted butter

1 medium yellow onion, peeled and finely diced

2 stalks celery, finely diced

2 cups diced ham steak

2 cloves garlic, peeled and minced

1 pound dried green split peas

6 cups Ham Stock or Chicken Stock (see recipes in Chapter 2)

1 bay leaf

½ teaspoon salt

½ teaspoon ground black pepper

1 Press the Sauté button on the Instant Pot® and melt butter. Add onion, celery, and ham. Sauté about 3 minutes. Add garlic and cook until fragrant, about 30 seconds. Press the Cancel button.

2 Add peas, stock, bay leaf, salt, and pepper to pot. Close lid, set steam release to Sealing, press the Manual button, and set time to 20 minutes. When the timer beeps, quick-release the pressure. Press the Cancel button, open lid, and discard bay leaf.

3 Purée one-third of the soup in a blender, then return to the pot and stir well. Serve hot.

PER SERVING

CALORIES: 331 | FAT: 10g | PROTEIN: 21g | SODIUM: 693mg
FIBER: 15g | CARBOHYDRATES: 39g | SUGAR: 5g

Cabbage and Bacon Soup

Cabbage is in season in the fall and winter, and during this time you will find plump, nutrient-rich heads of cabbage that have an almost sweet flavor. If you are making this soup in the spring or summer, you may need to use two heads of cabbage as they are smaller in the warmer months.

- **Hands-On Time: 20 minutes**
- **Cook Time: 3 minutes**

Serves 8

2 tablespoons vegetable oil

8 slices thick-cut bacon, chopped

2 medium yellow onions, peeled and chopped

1 large head cabbage, cored and chopped

2 cloves garlic, peeled and minced

4 cups Vegetable Broth (see recipe in Chapter 2)

1 cup Bone Broth (see recipe in Chapter 2)

¼ teaspoon crushed red pepper flakes

½ teaspoon salt

½ teaspoon ground black pepper

1. Press the Sauté button on the Instant Pot® and heat oil. Add bacon and cook until just starting to brown around the edges, about 8 minutes. Add onions and cook until tender, about 5 minutes. Add cabbage and garlic and cook until fragrant, about 1 minute. Press the Cancel button.

2. Add broths and red pepper flakes. Stir well, close lid, set steam release to Sealing, press the Manual button, and set time to 3 minutes.

3. When the timer beeps, let pressure release naturally, about 20–25 minutes. Open lid and season with salt and pepper. Serve hot.

PER SERVING

CALORIES: 224 | **FAT:** 16g | **PROTEIN:** 7g | **SODIUM:** 374mg
FIBER: 4g | **CARBOHYDRATES:** 13g | **SUGAR:** 6g

FREEZING SOUP

You can freeze most soups. Broth-based soups, bean or lentil soups, chilis, and stews are all prime candidates for the freezer. Cream-based soups and cheese soups do not always freeze as well. Divide the soup into individual containers and freeze for an easy lunch or dinner for one.

4

Cream Soups

Cream soups are incredibly versatile. They are a warm and filling meal on a cold night, they make a lovely first course for an elegant dinner, and they can be used as a base for other recipes like casseroles. Some cream soups are enriched with cream at the end of cooking, while others are made creamy through the puréeing of vegetables. They can be served chunky or silky smooth, and can be simple, made with just vegetables or cheese, or complex with layered flavors, meats, and grains.

With the Instant Pot® you can create cream soups with less of the active work that the traditional versions require. On the stove, a cream soup requires a fair bit of babysitting and time, but in the Instant Pot® cream soups are ready in mere minutes. When you want the comfort of a creamy soup, you won't have long to wait!

Cream of Chicken Soup

This most classic of cream soups is as elegant as it is filling. You can serve this soup three ways. First, very chunky with large pieces of meat and vegetable. Second, with small pieces of meat and vegetable, as in this recipe. Third, you can cook the soup without the meat, purée the vegetables until smooth, then fold in the chicken pieces with the cream at the end of cooking.

- **Hands-On Time: 15 minutes**
- **Cook Time: 1 minute**

Serves 8

3 tablespoons unsalted butter

3 stalks celery, finely chopped

2 medium carrots, peeled and finely chopped

½ medium onion, peeled and finely chopped

1 clove garlic, peeled and minced

¼ teaspoon poultry seasoning

1 bay leaf

½ teaspoon salt

¼ teaspoon ground black pepper

3 tablespoons all-purpose flour

½ cup white wine

4 cups Chicken Broth (see recipe in Chapter 2) or water

3 cups finely chopped cooked chicken breast

1 cup whole milk

½ cup heavy whipping cream

3 tablespoons chopped fresh flat-leaf parsley

1 Press the Sauté button on the Instant Pot® and melt butter. Add celery, carrots, and onion. Cook until tender, about 8 minutes, then add garlic, poultry seasoning, bay leaf, salt, and pepper. Cook until fragrant, about 1 minute.

2 Add flour and cook for 1 minute, making sure all flour is moistened. Press the Cancel button, add wine, and cook, scraping the bottom of the pot well. Slowly add broth and chicken. Mix well. Close lid, set steam release to Sealing, press the Manual button, and set time for 1 minute.

3 When the timer beeps, let pressure release naturally for 10 minutes, then quick-release the remaining pressure. Press the Cancel button and open lid. Remove bay leaf, stir in milk and cream, and top with parsley. Serve hot.

PER SERVING

CALORIES: 233 | **FAT:** 12g | **PROTEIN:** 19g | **SODIUM:** 230mg
FIBER: 1g | **CARBOHYDRATES:** 7g | **SUGAR:** 3g

Cream of Jalapeño Soup

Here's an unexpected way of using jalapeño peppers. For a soup with less spice, you can carefully scrape out the ribs of the jalapeños before chopping. If you want a soup with more kick, add a few dashes of your favorite hot sauce.

- **Hands-On Time: 15 minutes**
- **Cook Time: 3 minutes**

Serves 8

4 tablespoons unsalted butter

8 medium jalapeño peppers, seeded and finely chopped

1 medium onion, peeled and finely chopped

3 cloves garlic, peeled and minced

½ teaspoon ground cumin

½ teaspoon ground coriander

½ teaspoon salt

¼ teaspoon ground black pepper

¼ teaspoon smoked paprika

¼ cup all-purpose flour

4 cups Chicken Broth (see recipe in Chapter 2)

¾ cup heavy whipping cream

1 Press the Sauté button on the Instant Pot® and melt butter. Add jalapeños and onion. Cook until tender, about 6 minutes, then add garlic, cumin, coriander, salt, black pepper, and paprika. Cook until fragrant, about 1 minute.

2 Add flour and cook for 1 minute, making sure all flour is moistened. Press the Cancel button, then slowly add broth and mix well, scraping the bottom of pot well. Close lid, set steam release to Sealing, press the Manual button, and set time for 3 minutes.

3 When the timer beeps, let pressure release naturally for 10 minutes, then quick-release the remaining pressure. Press the Cancel button, open lid, and stir soup well. Purée with an immersion blender or blend soup in batches in a blender. Stir in cream. Serve hot.

PER SERVING

CALORIES: 163 | FAT: 14g | PROTEIN: 2g | SODIUM: 159mg
FIBER: 1g | CARBOHYDRATES: 6g | SUGAR: 2g

Creamy Celery Soup

Celery has a surprising amount of flavor, and it shines when cooked into this creamy soup. If you prefer a thicker soup, simmer the soup on the Low Sauté setting for 10–20 minutes before adding the cream, stirring frequently, until it reaches the thickness you prefer.

- **Hands-On Time: 20 minutes**
- **Cook Time: 1 minute**

Serves 8

4 tablespoons unsalted butter

6 stalks celery, diced

1 medium onion, peeled and diced

1 clove garlic, peeled and minced

¼ teaspoon dried dill

½ teaspoon salt

¼ teaspoon ground black pepper

¼ cup all-purpose flour

4 cups Chicken Broth (see recipe in Chapter 2)

½ cup heavy whipping cream

1 Press the Sauté button and melt butter. Add celery and onion. Cook until tender, about 8 minutes, then add garlic, dill, salt, and pepper. Cook until fragrant, about 1 minute.

2 Add flour and cook for 1 minute, making sure all flour is moistened. Press the Cancel button, then slowly add broth and mix well, scraping the bottom of pot well. Close lid, set steam release to Sealing, press the Manual button, and set time for 1 minute.

3 When the timer beeps, let pressure release naturally for 10 minutes, then quick-release the remaining pressure. Press the Cancel button and open lid. Purée soup with an immersion blender or blend soup in batches in a blender. Stir in cream. Serve hot.

PER SERVING

CALORIES: 134 | FAT: 11g | PROTEIN: 2g | SODIUM: 638mg
FIBER: 1g | CARBOHYDRATES: 6g | SUGAR: 2g

Creamed Potato Leek Soup

Leeks can be gritty if not properly cleaned. To ensure all the grit is removed, soak the sliced leeks in cold water for 10 minutes, gently swishing the leeks for a few seconds at the start of soaking. The grit should sink to the bottom of the bowl.

- **Hands-On Time: 20 minutes**
- **Cook Time: 20 minutes**

Serves 8

4 tablespoons unsalted butter

2 medium leeks, thinly sliced

4 large russet potatoes, peeled and diced

1 clove garlic, minced

½ teaspoon dried thyme

½ teaspoon salt

1 bay leaf

¼ teaspoon ground black pepper

4 cups Chicken Broth (see recipe in Chapter 2)

1 cup heavy whipping cream

¼ cup sliced scallions

DAIRY-FREE CREAM ALTERNATIVE

For a dairy-free cream soup, use a vegan alternative to cream. Soak 1 cup raw cashews in ³/₄ cup filtered water for 4 hours. Purée in a blender until smooth, adding more water if needed to reach your preferred consistency. Season with ¼ teaspoon sea salt and add a drop or two of lemon juice or apple cider vinegar to give it a little extra tang.

1. Press the Sauté button on the Instant Pot® and melt butter. Add leeks and cook until tender, about 8 minutes, then add potatoes, garlic, thyme, salt, bay leaf, and pepper. Cook until fragrant, about 1 minute.

2. Press the Cancel button, then slowly add broth and mix well. Close lid, set steam release to Sealing, press the Soup button, and cook for the default time of 20 minutes.

3. When the timer beeps, let pressure release naturally for 10 minutes, then quick-release the remaining pressure. Press the Cancel button, open lid, remove bay leaf, and purée soup with an immersion blender or blend soup in batches in a blender. Once smooth stir in cream. Serve hot with scallions for garnish.

PER SERVING

CALORIES: 251 | FAT: 16g | PROTEIN: 4g | SODIUM: 170mg
FIBER: 2g | CARBOHYDRATES: 21g | SUGAR: 3g

Cream of Mushroom Soup

This creamy mushroom soup makes a hearty meal alone, and is great if you are feeling under the weather. If you are able to find fresh wild mushrooms you can use them here, or use whatever fresh mushrooms are available in your produce market. If you don't have Mushroom Stock on hand, you can use the same amount of water.

- **Hands-On Time: 20 minutes**
- **Cook Time: 5 minutes**

Serves 8

3 tablespoons unsalted butter

1 medium carrot, peeled and finely chopped

1 stalk celery, finely chopped

½ medium onion, peeled and finely chopped

1 clove garlic, peeled and minced

2 pounds sliced button or baby bella mushrooms

2 tablespoons sherry

4 cups Mushroom Stock (see recipe in Chapter 2)

1 cup water

1 tablespoon chopped fresh tarragon

½ teaspoon salt

½ teaspoon ground black pepper

¾ cup heavy whipping cream

1 Press the Sauté button on the Instant Pot® and melt butter. Add carrot, celery, and onion. Cook, stirring often, until softened, about 5 minutes. Add garlic and cook until fragrant, about 30 seconds, then add mushrooms and cook until they just begin to soften, about 5 minutes. Press the Cancel button.

2 Add sherry, stock, water, tarragon, salt, and pepper and stir well. Close lid, set steam release to Sealing, press the Manual button, and set time to 5 minutes. Once cooking is complete allow pressure to release naturally, about 10–15 minutes. Press the Cancel button, open lid, and stir. Purée soup with immersion blender or in batches in a blender. Stir in cream. Serve hot.

PER SERVING

CALORIES: 159 | FAT: 13g | PROTEIN: 5g | SODIUM: 181mg
FIBER: 2g | CARBOHYDRATES: 7g | SUGAR: 4g

Creamy Asparagus Soup with Basil

Asparagus has a delicate, earthy flavor that is enhanced by the fresh green flavor of basil. The Instant Pot® helps to break down the asparagus, making it easier to purée into a silky-smooth soup. For a fancy garnish, top each bowl with two or three cooked asparagus tips and a drizzle of cream.

- **Hands-On Time: 15 minutes**
- **Cook Time: 5 minutes**

Serves 8

4 tablespoons unsalted butter

2 cups chopped asparagus

1 stalk celery, chopped

1 medium onion, peeled and chopped

1 clove garlic, peeled and minced

3 tablespoons chopped fresh basil

½ teaspoon salt

¼ teaspoon ground black pepper

¼ cup all-purpose flour

4 cups Chicken Broth (see recipe in Chapter 2) or water

1 cup whole milk

¾ cup heavy whipping cream

1 Press the Sauté button on the Instant Pot® and melt butter. Add asparagus, celery, and onion. Cook until tender, about 5 minutes, then add garlic, basil, salt, and pepper. Cook until fragrant, about 1 minute.

2 Add flour and cook for 1 minute, making sure all flour is moistened. Press the Cancel button, then slowly add broth and mix well, scraping the bottom of pot well. Close lid, set steam release to Sealing, press the Manual button, and set time for 5 minutes.

3 When the timer beeps, let pressure release naturally for 10 minutes, then quick-release the remaining pressure. Press the Cancel button, open lid, and stir in milk. Purée soup with an immersion blender or blend soup in batches in a blender. Stir in cream. Serve hot.

PER SERVING

CALORIES: 184 | **FAT:** 15g | **PROTEIN:** 4g | **SODIUM:** 176mg **FIBER:** 1g | **CARBOHYDRATES:** 8g | **SUGAR:** 3g

Beer Cheese Soup

Lager- or ale-style beers are best for this soup because they don't overpower the flavor of the cheese, but instead enhance it with a mildly bitter and nutty flavor. Garnish bowls of this soup with chopped crisp bacon or finely sliced scallions.

- **Hands-On Time: 20 minutes**
- **Cook Time: 5 minutes**

Serves 8

3 tablespoons unsalted butter

2 medium carrots, peeled and chopped

2 stalks celery, chopped

1 medium onion, peeled and chopped

1 clove garlic, peeled and minced

1 teaspoon dried mustard

½ teaspoon smoked paprika

¼ cup all-purpose flour

1 (12-ounce) bottle lager beer or ale

4 cups Chicken Broth (see recipe in Chapter 2)

½ cup heavy cream

2 cups shredded sharp Cheddar cheese

1 cup shredded smoked Gouda cheese

1. Press the Sauté button on the Instant Pot® and melt butter. Add carrots, celery, and onion. Cook, stirring often, until softened, about 5 minutes. Add garlic and cook until fragrant, about 30 seconds, then add mustard and paprika and stir well.

2. Add flour and stir well to combine, then cook for 1 minute. Slowly stir in beer, scraping the bottom of pot well, then add broth. Press the Cancel button.

3. Close lid, set steam release to Sealing, press the Manual button, and set time to 5 minutes. When the timer beeps, let pressure release naturally, about 15 minutes. Open lid and purée mixture with an immersion blender. Stir in cream, then stir in cheese 1 cup at a time, whisking each addition until completely melted before adding another. Serve hot.

PER SERVING

CALORIES: 302 | FAT: 22g | PROTEIN: 13g | SODIUM: 319mg
FIBER: 1g | CARBOHYDRATES: 8g | SUGAR: 2g

Wisconsin Cheese Soup

This cheese soup is both silky and chunky at the same time, with a creamy cheese soup base and tender bits of vegetables. It's great with hot ham or turkey and cheese sandwiches, alongside a green salad, or all alone with a garnish of hot sauce.

- **Hands-On Time: 20 minutes**
- **Cook Time: 5 minutes**

Serves 8

3 tablespoons unsalted butter

3 medium carrots, peeled and finely chopped

2 stalks celery, finely chopped

1 medium onion, peeled and finely chopped

1 clove garlic, peeled and minced

1 teaspoon dried mustard

¼ teaspoon paprika

¼ cup all-purpose flour

4 cups Chicken Broth (see recipe in Chapter 2)

1 cup heavy cream

2 cups shredded sharp Cheddar cheese

1 cup shredded American cheese

1   Press the Sauté button on the Instant Pot® and melt butter. Add carrots, celery, and onion. Cook, stirring often, until softened, about 5 minutes. Add garlic and cook until fragrant, about 30 seconds, then add mustard and paprika and stir well.

2   Add flour and stir well to combine, then cook for 1 minute. Slowly stir in broth, scraping the bottom of pot well. Press the Cancel button.

3   Close lid, set steam release to Sealing, press the Manual button, and set time to 5 minutes. When the timer beeps, let pressure release naturally, about 15 minutes. Open lid and stir soup well. Stir in cream, then stir in cheeses 1 cup at a time, whisking each addition until completely melted before adding another. Serve hot.

PER SERVING

CALORIES: 341 | FAT: 26g | PROTEIN: 13g | SODIUM: 416mg
FIBER: 1g | CARBOHYDRATES: 10g | SUGAR: 4g

Cream of Broccoli Soup

If you're a fan of broccoli, you'll love this soup! The Instant Pot® helps preserve the flavor and nutrients of the broccoli as it cooks, so you will have maximum flavor and nutrition.

- **Hands-On Time: 15 minutes**
- **Cook Time: 15 minutes**

Serves 6

3 tablespoons unsalted butter

1 medium carrot, peeled and finely chopped

1 stalk celery, finely chopped

1 medium onion, peeled and finely chopped

2 cloves garlic, peeled and minced

4 cups chopped broccoli florets

¼ cup all-purpose flour

2 cups Vegetable Broth or Chicken Broth (see recipes in Chapter 2)

2 cups whole milk

½ cup heavy cream

1 Press the Sauté button on the Instant Pot® and melt butter. Add carrot, celery, and onion. Cook, stirring often, until softened, about 5 minutes. Add garlic and cook until fragrant, about 30 seconds, then add broccoli and stir well.

2 Add flour and stir well to combine, then cook for 1 minute. Slowly stir in broth, scraping the bottom of pot well. Press the Cancel button.

3 Close lid, set steam release to Sealing, press the Manual button, and set time to 5 minutes. When the timer beeps, let pressure release naturally, about 15 minutes. Press the Cancel button, open lid, stir in milk, and then purée mixture with an immersion blender, or in batches in a blender, until smooth. Press the Sauté button and let soup simmer for 10 minutes to thicken. Press the Cancel button. Stir in cream. Serve hot.

PER SERVING

CALORIES: 228 | FAT: 15g | PROTEIN: 6g | SODIUM: 77mg
FIBER: 2g | CARBOHYDRATES: 16g | SUGAR: 7g

Creamy Vidalia Onion Soup

Vidalia onions have a naturally sweeter flavor than standard white, yellow, or red onions. In this soup, they add a natural sweetness along with the savory onion flavor. The Instant Pot® helps break down the onions as they cook, releasing more of the sweet flavor that pairs perfectly with the cream you stir in at the end.

- **Hands-On Time: 20 minutes**
- **Cook Time: 3 minutes**

Serves 8

4 tablespoons unsalted butter
2 large Vidalia onions, peeled and diced
1 stalk celery, diced
1 clove garlic, peeled and minced
¼ teaspoon dried thyme
½ teaspoon salt
¼ teaspoon ground black pepper
3 tablespoons all-purpose flour
4 cups Chicken Broth (see recipe in Chapter 2)
1 cup whole milk
¾ cup heavy whipping cream

1 Press the Sauté button on the Instant Pot® and melt butter. Add onions and celery. Cook until very tender, about 12 minutes, then add garlic, thyme, salt, and pepper. Cook until fragrant, about 1 minute.

2 Add flour and cook for 1 minute. Press the Cancel button, then slowly add broth and mix well. Close lid, set steam release to Sealing, press the Manual button, and set time for 3 minutes.

3 When the timer beeps, let pressure release naturally for 10 minutes, then quick-release the remaining pressure. Press the Cancel button, open lid, and stir in milk. Purée soup with an immersion blender or in batches in a blender. Stir in cream. Serve hot.

PER SERVING

CALORIES: 183 | FAT: 15g | PROTEIN: 3g | SODIUM: 176mg
FIBER: 1g | CARBOHYDRATES: 8g | SUGAR: 4g

Cream of Fennel Soup

Fennel has a slight licorice flavor that mellows as it cooks. It has a number of health benefits, and is a good source of potassium, vitamin A, and minerals essential to bone health. It is also thought that fennel can help lower blood pressure due to its magnesium, potassium, and calcium content. So enjoy your soup knowing you are doing your body good!

- **Hands-On Time: 20 minutes**
- **Cook Time: 3 minutes**

Serves 8

2 tablespoons unsalted butter

2 bulbs fennel, tops trimmed and bulbs diced

2 stalks celery, diced

1 medium onion, peeled and chopped

1 clove garlic, peeled and minced

½ teaspoon dried dill

½ teaspoon salt

¼ teaspoon ground black pepper

¼ cup all-purpose flour

4 cups Chicken Broth (see recipe in Chapter 2)

1 cup heavy whipping cream

1. Press the Sauté button on the Instant Pot® and melt butter. Add fennel, celery, and onion. Cook until tender, about 8 minutes, then add garlic, dill, salt, and pepper. Cook until fragrant, about 1 minute.

2. Add flour and cook for 1 minute, making sure all flour is moistened. Press the Cancel button, then slowly add broth and mix well, scraping the bottom of pot well. Close lid, set steam release to Sealing, press the Manual button, and set time for 3 minutes.

3. When the timer beeps, let pressure release naturally for 10 minutes, then quick-release the remaining pressure. Press the Cancel button, open lid, and purée soup with an immersion blender or in batches in a blender. Stir in cream. Serve hot.

PER SERVING

CALORIES: 172 | FAT: 14g | PROTEIN: 3g | SODIUM: 199mg
FIBER: 2g | CARBOHYDRATES: 9g | SUGAR: 3g

Creamy Pea Soup with Lemon

Frozen peas are picked and frozen at the peak of freshness, so even in the colder months you can enjoy a little taste of spring! The addition of lemon adds a bright, slightly sharp edge to the sweetness of the peas.

- **Hands-On Time: 15 minutes**
- **Cook Time: 4 minutes**

Serves 8

2 tablespoons olive oil

1 medium onion, peeled and finely chopped

1 stalk celery, finely chopped

1 clove garlic, minced

½ teaspoon salt

¼ teaspoon black pepper

1 tablespoon grated lemon zest

2 pounds fresh or frozen green peas

4 cups Chicken Broth (see recipe in Chapter 2)

½ cup heavy whipping cream

ALTERNATIVE WAYS TO THICKEN SOUPS

You can thicken cream soups without flour. Stir in a slurry made of equal parts cornstarch and water at the end. Simmer the soup until thickened. Or, if you have time, simmer the soup on the Sauté setting adjusted to Low for 20–30 minutes. The soup will thicken naturally. If you use this method, season the soup after thickening, starting with a quarter of the salt.

1 Press the Sauté button on the Instant Pot® and heat oil. Add onion and celery. Cook until just tender, about 5 minutes. Add garlic, salt, and pepper and cook until fragrant, about 30 seconds. Add lemon zest and peas and turn to coat. Press the Cancel button.

2 Add broth and stir well. Close lid, set steam release to Sealing, press the Manual button, and adjust time to 4 minutes. When the timer beeps, let pressure release naturally, about 20–25 minutes. Press the Cancel button and open lid. Purée soup with an immersion blender or in batches in a blender. Stir in cream. Serve hot.

PER SERVING

CALORIES: 189 | FAT: 9g | PROTEIN: 8g | SODIUM: 165mg
FIBER: 6g | CARBOHYDRATES: 19g | SUGAR: 8g

Creamy Chicken and Chive Soup

Chives have a mild flavor that is a cross between onion and garlic. When you cook the chives into the broth you extract a lot of flavor, and it serves to enhance the chicken and cream here. If you can't find fresh chives, you can use freeze-dried chives in equal amounts, or half the amount of dried chives.

- **Hands-On Time: 15 minutes**
- **Cook Time: 1 minute**

Serves 8

3 tablespoons unsalted butter

2 stalks celery, finely chopped

1 medium carrot, peeled and finely chopped

½ medium onion, peeled and finely chopped

⅓ cup chopped fresh chives, divided

1 tablespoon chopped fresh tarragon

1 clove garlic, peeled and minced

1 bay leaf

½ teaspoon salt

¼ teaspoon ground black pepper

¼ cup all-purpose flour

⅓ cup white wine

4 cups Chicken Broth (see recipe in Chapter 2) or water

2 cups diced cooked chicken breast

1 cup whole milk

¾ cup heavy whipping cream

1 Press the Sauté button on the Instant Pot® and melt butter. Add celery, carrot, and onion. Cook until tender, about 8 minutes, then add ¼ cup chives, tarragon, garlic, bay leaf, salt, and pepper. Cook until fragrant, about 1 minute.

2 Add flour and cook for 1 minute, making sure all flour is moistened. Press the Cancel button, add wine, and cook, scraping the bottom of the pot well, then slowly add broth and mix well. Add chicken. Close lid, set steam release to Sealing, press the Manual button, and set time for 1 minute.

3 When the timer beeps, let pressure release naturally for 10 minutes, then quick-release the remaining pressure. Press the Cancel button and open lid. Remove bay leaf, stir in milk and cream, then serve with reserved chives for garnish.

PER SERVING

CALORIES: 228 | **FAT:** 14g | **PROTEIN:** 14g | **SODIUM:** 210mg
FIBER: 1g | **CARBOHYDRATES:** 7g | **SUGAR:** 3g

Steak and Potato Soup

Part luscious cream soup, part hearty stew, this soup is a full meal sure to be a comfort food favorite. Chicken thighs can be substituted for the beef, or you could eliminate the meat altogether: For a vegetarian soup, replace the beef with mushrooms and use Roasted Vegetable Stock (see recipe in Chapter 2) in place of the Beef Stock.

- **Hands-On Time: 25 minutes**
- **Cook Time: 20 minutes**

Serves 8

1 pound beef chuck, cut into 1" pieces

⅓ cup all-purpose flour, divided

4 tablespoons vegetable oil, divided

2 stalks celery, sliced

1 medium onion, peeled and chopped

2 cloves garlic, peeled and minced

½ teaspoon salt

¼ teaspoon ground black pepper

4 cups Beef Stock (see recipe in Chapter 2)

2 pounds russet potatoes, peeled and cut into 1" pieces

1 cup whole milk

1 cup heavy whipping cream

1 In a large zip-top plastic bag add beef and ¼ cup flour. Seal bag and shake to coat beef pieces. Set aside.

2 Press the Sauté button on the Instant Pot® and heat 2 tablespoons oil. Add beef in two batches, browning well on both sides, about 3 minutes per side. Transfer beef to a plate and repeat until all beef is browned.

3 Add reserved oil to pot. Add celery and onion and sauté until tender, about 8 minutes, then add garlic, salt, and pepper. Cook until fragrant, about 1 minute.

4 Add reserved flour and cook for 1 minute, making sure all flour is moistened. Press the Cancel button, then slowly add stock and mix well, scraping the bottom of pot well. Add beef and potatoes, then close lid, set steam release to Sealing, press the Soup button, and cook for the default time of 20 minutes.

5 When the timer beeps, let pressure release naturally for 10 minutes, then quick-release the remaining pressure. Press the Cancel button, open lid, and stir in milk and cream. Serve hot.

PER SERVING

CALORIES: 385 | FAT: 21g | PROTEIN: 18g | SODIUM: 237mg
FIBER: 2g | CARBOHYDRATES: 29g | SUGAR: 5g

Roasted Garlic and Potato Soup

Roasted garlic has a mild, sweet flavor and a caramelized brown color. Oven roasting is the best way to prepare the garlic at home, and can be done up to five days in advance. Roasted garlic can be found in jars at the market, but it's easy to make yourself at home. You will be rewarded with amazing flavor if you do.

- **Hands-On Time: 15 minutes**
- **Cook Time: 20 minutes**

Serves 8

4 tablespoons unsalted butter

1 medium onion, peeled and finely chopped

1 bulb roasted garlic (see sidebar)

5 pounds russet potatoes, peeled and diced

½ teaspoon dried thyme

½ teaspoon salt

1 bay leaf

¼ teaspoon black pepper

4 cups Chicken Broth (see recipe in Chapter 2) or water

1 cup heavy whipping cream

¼ cup sliced scallions

1 Press the Sauté button on the Instant Pot® and melt butter. Add onion and garlic. Cook until onion is tender, about 8 minutes, then add potatoes, thyme, salt, bay leaf, and pepper. Cook until fragrant, about 1 minute.

2 Press the Cancel button, then slowly add broth and mix well. Close lid, set steam release to Sealing, press the Soup button, and cook for the default time of 20 minutes.

3 When the timer beeps, let pressure release naturally for 10 minutes, then quick-release the remaining pressure. Press the Cancel button, open lid, and remove bay leaf. Purée soup with an immersion blender or blend soup in batches in a blender. Stir in cream. Serve hot with scallions for garnish.

PER SERVING

CALORIES: 387 | FAT: 17g | PROTEIN: 8g | SODIUM: 176mg
FIBER: 4g | CARBOHYDRATES: 52g | SUGAR: 3g

ROASTING GARLIC

To roast a bulb of garlic, slice off the top, drizzle it with olive oil, and sprinkle with ¼ teaspoon sea salt. Wrap tightly in aluminum foil and roast at 400°F for 30–40 minutes, or until the cloves are tender and golden brown. Remove from oven, unwrap, and allow the bulb to cool before squeezing the garlic from the bulb.

Wild Rice Soup

Be it a cold and rainy day or a lazy weekend with family, this hearty and filling soup is sure to please. You can make a vegan version by substituting olive oil for the butter, replacing the Chicken Broth with a vegetable or mushroom stock, and omitting the cream.

- **Hands-On Time: 15 minutes**
- **Cook Time: 48 minutes**

Serves 8

2 tablespoons unsalted butter

4 medium carrots, peeled and chopped

4 stalks celery, chopped

1 medium onion, peeled and chopped

1 (8-ounce) container sliced mushrooms

2 cloves garlic, peeled and minced

½ teaspoon dried thyme

1 teaspoon salt

½ teaspoon black pepper

1 cup uncooked wild rice

4 cups Chicken Broth (see recipe in Chapter 2)

⅓ cup water

2 tablespoons cornstarch

½ cup heavy cream

WHAT IS WILD RICE?

Like white rice, wild rice is the seed of an aquatic grass. Wild rice is high in protein and fiber and low in fat. It's a good source of lysine, an amino acid that is good for your brain and gut.

1 Press the Sauté button on the Instant Pot® and melt butter. Add carrots, celery, and onion. Cook until vegetables are just tender, about 4–5 minutes, then add mushrooms and cook until they start to release liquid, about 3 minutes.

2 Add garlic, thyme, salt, pepper, and rice and cook until garlic is fragrant, about 1 minute. Press the Cancel button, add broth, and close lid. Set steam release to Sealing, press the Manual button, and set time to 45 minutes.

3 When the timer beeps, quick-release the pressure, open lid, and stir well. Press the Cancel button, then press the Sauté button. Whisk together water and cornstarch and stir into pot. Bring to a boil, stirring constantly, until thickened, about 3–4 minutes. Press the Cancel button and stir in cream. Serve hot.

PER SERVING

CALORIES: 194 | FAT: 9g | PROTEIN: 6g | SODIUM: 341mg
FIBER: 3g | CARBOHYDRATES: 23g | SUGAR: 4g

Creamy Turkey and Wild Rice Soup

While this recipe calls for turkey breast, you can use any parts of the turkey you may have on hand. Reserved wings, thighs, back, or even a couple of turkey necks will work. You can also omit the raw turkey, cook the soup per the instructions, and when you stir in the cream add 2 cups of chopped leftover cooked turkey.

- **Hands-On Time: 20 minutes**
- **Cook Time: 48 minutes**

Serves 8

2 tablespoons unsalted butter

2 medium carrots, peeled and chopped

2 stalks celery, chopped

1 medium onion, peeled and chopped

2 cloves garlic, peeled and minced

1 teaspoon poultry seasoning

1 teaspoon salt

½ teaspoon ground black pepper

1 cup uncooked wild rice

1 (6-pound) bone-in turkey breast, skin removed

4 cups Turkey Stock (see recipe in Chapter 2)

⅓ cup water

2 tablespoons cornstarch

½ cup heavy cream

1 Press the Sauté button on the Instant Pot® and melt butter. Add carrots, celery, and onion. Cook until vegetables are just tender, about 4–5 minutes, then add garlic, poultry seasoning, salt, pepper, and rice and cook until garlic is fragrant, about 1 minute.

2 Add turkey breast to pot and toss to coat. Press the Cancel button, add stock, close lid, set steam release to Sealing, press the Manual button, and set time to 45 minutes.

3 When the timer beeps, quick-release the pressure, open lid, and stir well. Press the Cancel button. Transfer turkey breast to a cutting board and allow to cool slightly, then shred meat, discarding bones. Return turkey to pot.

4 Press the Sauté button. Whisk together water and cornstarch and stir into pot. Bring to a boil, stirring constantly, until thickened, about 3–4 minutes. Press the Cancel button and stir in cream. Serve hot.

PER SERVING

CALORIES: 443 | FAT: 10g | PROTEIN: 62g | SODIUM: 864mg
FIBER: 2g | CARBOHYDRATES: 22g | SUGAR: 3g

Beans and Lentils

Lentils and beans are members of the legume family. Rich in protein, naturally gluten-free, and high in fiber and essential nutrients, beans and lentils are a healthy and filling choice you can feel good about. And if you use any of the wide variety of dried beans and lentils available at your local grocer, you'll also stretch your food budget.

The Instant Pot® takes the stress and worry out of bean and lentil preparation. Lentils need no special preparation other than rinsing. Easy-peasy! Dried beans can be prepared in one of two ways. You can soak them overnight in water or you can add the dried beans directly to the Instant Pot®.

Presoaking decreases the cooking time, and it yields a prettier bean once cooked. Using unsoaked beans adds only an additional 10–15 minutes to the cooking time, so it's a great solution when you do not have soaked beans on hand. Remember, dried beans double in volume when cooking, so you may need to add additional liquid after cooking.

When cooking in the Instant Pot® is complete, it's best to let the pressure in the pot release naturally. This will allow for a more tender bean or lentil.

Loaded Vegetable and Lentil Stew

When the weather turns cold and you feel chilled to your bones, turn to this stew to warm you up inside and out! For a Tex-Mex flavor, replace the oregano and fennel with ½ teaspoon cumin and ½ teaspoon chili powder and use a can of diced tomatoes with green chilies instead of plain diced tomatoes.

- **Hands-On Time: 5 minutes**
- **Cook Time: 25 minutes**

Serves 6

2 tablespoons olive oil

2 stalks celery, sliced

2 medium carrots, peeled and sliced

1 medium yellow onion, peeled and chopped

2 cloves garlic, minced

½ teaspoon dried oregano

¼ teaspoon ground fennel

½ teaspoon salt

2 cups green lentils

1 medium sweet potato, peeled and diced

1 (15-ounce) can diced tomatoes, drained

4 cups Roasted Vegetable Stock (see recipe in Chapter 2)

1 Press the Sauté button on the Instant Pot® and heat oil. Add celery, carrots, and onion and cook until just tender, about 3 minutes. Add garlic, oregano, fennel, and salt. Cook until fragrant, about 30 seconds. Press the Cancel button.

2 Add lentils, sweet potato, tomatoes, and stock. Close lid, set steam release to Sealing, press the Manual button, and adjust time to 25 minutes. When the timer beeps, let pressure release naturally, about 15 minutes. Remove lid and stir. Serve warm.

PER SERVING

CALORIES: 345 | FAT: 8g | PROTEIN: 17g | SODIUM: 366mg
FIBER: 10g | CARBOHYDRATES: 54g | SUGAR: 8g

COLORFUL LENTILS

Lentil varieties, including beluga, French green, Red Chief, and Spanish brown grow best in cooler climates. They are grown in Canada, which is the global leader in lentil production, and some northern states in the US, such as Washington and Idaho.

Curried Lentil Soup

The earthy flavor of lentils is enhanced by garam masala and red curry paste, made creamy with coconut milk. Most grocery stores carry red curry paste, but if you are unable to locate it you can substitute a tablespoon of red curry powder mixed with a teaspoon of vegetable oil.

- **Hands-On Time: 10 minutes**
- **Cook Time: 15 minutes**

Serves 6

2 tablespoons salted butter

1 medium white onion, peeled and chopped

1 tablespoon red curry paste

½ teaspoon garam masala

½ teaspoon turmeric

½ teaspoon brown sugar

2 cloves garlic, minced

2 teaspoons grated fresh ginger

3 tablespoons tomato paste

1 cup red lentils

4 cups Chicken Stock or Vegetable Broth (see recipes in Chapter 2)

½ cup full-fat canned coconut milk, shaken well

1 Press the Sauté button on the Instant Pot® and melt butter. Add onion and cook until just tender, about 3 minutes. Add curry paste, garam masala, turmeric, brown sugar, garlic, and ginger and cook until fragrant, about 30 seconds. Stir in tomato paste and cook for 30 seconds. Press the Cancel button.

2 Add lentils and stock, close lid, set steam release to Sealing, press the Manual button, and adjust time to 15 minutes. When the timer beeps, let pressure release naturally, about 15 minutes. Remove lid and stir in coconut milk. Serve warm.

PER SERVING

CALORIES: 220 | FAT: 9g | PROTEIN: 10g | SODIUM: 142mg
FIBER: 4g | CARBOHYDRATES: 26g | SUGAR: 2g

ANCIENT PULSES

Lentils are among the oldest recorded pulse crops domesticated by man, with evidence that ancient Romans and Egyptians cultivated them as a food crop. Today lentils are more popular than ever—they're easy to grow, inexpensive, highly nutritious, and packed with flavor.

Beef and Lentil Soup

Lentils are a great way to make smaller amounts of meat feed a larger crowd.

- **Hands-On Time: 15 minutes**
- **Cook Time: 25 minutes**

Serves 6

2 tablespoons olive oil

1 pound beef stew meat

2 stalks celery, chopped

1 medium onion, chopped

1 medium carrot, chopped

2 cloves garlic, minced

½ teaspoon salt

2 cups red lentils

1 large sweet potato, peeled and diced

2 cups Chicken Stock (see recipe in Chapter 2)

1 Press the Sauté button on the Instant Pot® and heat oil. Add beef and cook, stirring often, until well browned, about 10 minutes. Add celery, onion, and carrot and cook until just tender, about 3 minutes. Add garlic and salt and cook until fragrant, about 30 seconds. Press the Cancel button.

2 Add lentils, sweet potato, and stock. Close lid, set steam release to Sealing, press the Manual button, and adjust time to 25 minutes. When the timer beeps, let pressure release naturally, about 15 minutes. Remove lid and stir. Serve warm.

PER SERVING

CALORIES: 423 | FAT: 10g | PROTEIN: 35g | SODIUM: 294mg
FIBER: 8g | CARBOHYDRATES: 48g | SUGAR: 3g

White Beans and Tomato Soup

This soup is wonderful for lovers of fresh tomatoes. Use any ripe tomatoes you prefer.

- **Hands-On Time: 10 minutes**
- **Cook Time: 30 minutes**

Serves 4

1 tablespoon vegetable oil

1 medium white onion, peeled and chopped

2 cloves garlic, minced

1 pound tomatoes, chopped

½ teaspoon dried sage

½ teaspoon black pepper

1 cup cannellini beans, soaked overnight and drained

4 cups Vegetable Broth (see recipe in Chapter 2)

1 teaspoon salt

1 Press the Sauté button on the Instant Pot® and heat oil. Add onion and cook until tender, about 5 minutes. Add garlic and cook until fragrant, about 1 minute. Add tomatoes and cook for 1 minute.

2 Press the Cancel button and add sage, pepper, beans, and broth. Close lid, set steam release to Sealing, press the Bean button, and cook for the default time of 30 minutes.

3 When the timer beeps, let pressure release naturally. Open lid, stir well, and season with salt. Serve hot.

PER SERVING

CALORIES: 143 | FAT: 8g | PROTEIN: 4g | SODIUM: 790mg
FIBER: 5g | CARBOHYDRATES: 18g | SUGAR: 4g

White Bean Soup with Ham and Onion

This soup is simple, but it's that simplicity that makes it special. The flavors of the beans and ham, and the slight sweetness from the brown sugar are addictive.

- **Hands-On Time: 5 minutes**
- **Cook Time: 20 minutes**

Serves 6

1 pound dried white beans

1 ham bone (about 2 pounds), meat removed

1 medium yellow onion, peeled and diced

1 clove garlic, peeled and minced

2 tablespoons brown sugar

3 cups diced ham

1 teaspoon salt

½ teaspoon ground black pepper

4 cups Chicken Broth (see recipe in Chapter 2)

1 tablespoon olive oil

1 Place beans in a large bowl and cover with water. Set aside to soak overnight, then drain and place in the Instant Pot®.

2 Add remaining ingredients to the pot. Close lid, set steam release to Sealing, press the Manual button, and adjust time to 20 minutes. When the timer beeps, let pressure release naturally, about 20 minutes.

3 Remove lid and stir well. Serve hot.

PER SERVING

CALORIES: 456 | FAT: 11g | PROTEIN: 32g | SODIUM: 1,189mg
FIBER: 15g | CARBOHYDRATES: 55g | SUGAR: 6g

QUICK-SOAKING BEANS

You can "quick-soak" dried beans in the Instant Pot®. Rinse beans and put them in the pot with 4 cups of water for every 1 cup of beans. Press the Sauté button and bring beans to a boil, then press the Cancel button and close the lid. Set steam release to Sealing, press the Manual button, and adjust cook time to 2 minutes. When the timer beeps, let pressure release naturally, and drain.

Green Lentil Soup

With a peppery taste, green lentils lend themselves well to hearty soups packed with vegetables.

- **Hands-On Time: 5 minutes**
- **Cook Time: 25 minutes**

Serves 6

2 tablespoons olive oil

1 stalk celery, chopped

1 medium yellow onion, peeled and chopped

1 medium carrot, chopped

2 cloves garlic, minced

½ teaspoon salt

2 cups green lentils

1 large russet potato, peeled and diced

4 cups Chicken Stock (see recipe in Chapter 2)

1 Press the Sauté button on the Instant Pot® and heat oil. Add celery, onion, and carrot and cook until just tender, about 3 minutes. Add garlic and salt and cook until fragrant, about 30 seconds. Press the Cancel button.

2 Add lentils, potato, and stock. Close lid, set steam release to Sealing, press the Manual button, and adjust time to 25 minutes. When the timer beeps, let pressure release naturally, about 15 minutes. Remove lid and stir. Serve warm.

PER SERVING

CALORIES: 329 | FAT: 6g | PROTEIN: 19g | SODIUM: 222mg
FIBER: 8g | CARBOHYDRATES: 49g | SUGAR: 3g

White Bean and Kale Soup (pictured)

If you are looking for a filling vegan soup that also packs a punch of good-for-you nutrition and can be used for meals all week long, look no further!

- **Hands-On Time: 5 minutes**
- **Cook Time: 20 minutes**

Serves 6

1 pound dried white beans

2 stalks celery, chopped

1 medium yellow onion, peeled and diced

1 clove garlic, minced

3 cups chopped kale

1 teaspoon salt

½ teaspoon black pepper

6 cups Vegetable Broth (see recipe in Chapter 2)

1 tablespoon olive oil

1 In a large bowl, soak beans overnight in water to cover. Drain and add to the Instant Pot®.

2 Add remaining ingredients to the Instant Pot®. Close lid, set steam release to Sealing, press the Manual button, and adjust time to 20 minutes. When the timer beeps, let pressure release naturally, about 20 minutes.

3 Remove lid and stir well. Serve hot.

PER SERVING

CALORIES: 316 | FAT: 6g | PROTEIN: 17g | SODIUM: 417mg
FIBER: 16g | CARBOHYDRATES: 51g | SUGAR: 3g

Shrimp and White Bean Soup

Adding the shrimp at the end of cooking will ensure they do not overcook. An easy visual check for doneness is how curled the shrimp are. If they're curled into C shapes, they're cooked. If, on the other hand, they're curled into O shapes, they're overcooked.

- **Hands-On Time: 15 minutes**
- **Cook Time: 35 minutes**

Serves 4

2 tablespoons unsalted butter

2 stalks celery, finely chopped

1 medium sweet onion, peeled and finely chopped

1 medium green bell pepper, seeded and finely chopped

1 clove garlic, peeled and minced

½ teaspoon seafood seasoning

½ teaspoon dried thyme

½ teaspoon ground black pepper

1 bay leaf

1 cup dried cannellini beans, soaked overnight in water to cover and drained

4 cups Chicken Broth (see recipe in Chapter 2)

1 pound small peeled and deveined shrimp

1 cup frozen or fresh corn kernels

¼ teaspoon hot sauce

1 Press the Sauté button on the Instant Pot® and melt butter. Add celery, onion, and green pepper and cook until just tender, about 5 minutes. Add garlic, seafood seasoning, thyme, black pepper, and bay leaf and cook until garlic is fragrant, about 1 minute.

2 Press the Cancel button and add beans and broth to pot. Close lid, set steam release to Sealing, press the Bean button, and cook for the default time of 30 minutes.

3 When the timer beeps, let pressure release naturally, about 15 minutes. Open lid, remove bay leaf, and stir in shrimp and corn. Press the Cancel button, then press the Sauté button and simmer until shrimp are opaque and curled into C shapes, about 5–8 minutes. Drizzle with hot sauce before serving.

PER SERVING

CALORIES: 272 | FAT: 9g | PROTEIN: 24g | SODIUM: 768mg
FIBER: 2g | CARBOHYDRATES: 22g | SUGAR: 3g

Black-Eyed Pea Soup with Ham

Looking for prosperity and good luck? Some believe that eating black-eyed peas on New Year's Day will bring you good luck for the year to come. While there is no guarantee that it will work, eating this soup on New Year's Day will certainly ensure you have a yummy meal, and that is certainly a good start to a new year!

- **Hands-On Time: 10 minutes**
- **Cook Time: 10 minutes**

Serves 6

2 tablespoons olive oil

2 stalks celery, chopped

1 medium carrot, peeled and chopped

1 medium yellow onion, peeled and chopped

2 cloves garlic, peeled and lightly crushed

½ teaspoon salt

2 cups diced smoked ham

1 pound dried black-eyed peas, soaked overnight in water to cover and drained

½ teaspoon dried thyme leaves

4 cups Ham Stock or Chicken Broth (see recipes in Chapter 2)

1 Press the Sauté button on the Instant Pot® and heat oil. Add celery, carrot, and onion to pot. Cook until vegetables are tender, about 5 minutes. Add garlic and salt and cook until fragrant, about 30 seconds. Press the Cancel button.

2 Add ham, black-eyed peas, thyme, and stock to pot. Close lid and set steam release to Sealing, then press the Manual button and adjust cook time to 10 minutes.

3 When the timer beeps, let pressure release naturally, about 15–20 minutes, then open lid and stir well. Serve hot.

PER SERVING

CALORIES: 203 | FAT: 9g | PROTEIN: 12g | SODIUM: 1,148mg
FIBER: 5g | CARBOHYDRATES: 18g | SUGAR: 4g

Yellow Lentil and Spinach Soup

Baby spinach has a natural sweetness that would be lost if the tender leaves were overcooked, so it is best to add them after cooking. The heat of the soup will wilt the spinach leaves without making them soggy or mushy. If you have other chopped greens on hand, such as kale or chard, you can use them here.

- **Hands-On Time: 10 minutes**
- **Cook Time: 25 minutes**

Serves 6

2 tablespoons olive oil

2 stalks celery, sliced

1 medium yellow onion, peeled and roughly chopped

1 medium carrot, peeled and sliced

2 cloves garlic, peeled and minced

1 teaspoon fresh minced ginger

½ teaspoon ground cumin

½ teaspoon ground turmeric

¼ teaspoon smoked paprika

½ teaspoon salt

2 cups dried yellow lentils

4 cups Roasted Vegetable Stock (see recipe in Chapter 2)

4 cups baby spinach

1 tablespoon lemon juice

1 Press the Sauté button on the Instant Pot® and heat oil. Add celery, onion, and carrot and cook until just tender, about 3 minutes. Add garlic, ginger, cumin, turmeric, paprika, and salt. Cook until fragrant, about 1 minute. Press the Cancel button.

2 Add lentils and stock to pot. Close lid, set steam release to Sealing, press the Manual button, and adjust time to 25 minutes. When the timer beeps, let pressure release naturally, about 15 minutes. Remove lid and stir in spinach and lemon juice. Close lid and let stand for 10 minutes. Serve warm.

PER SERVING

CALORIES: 312 | FAT: 8g | PROTEIN: 17g | SODIUM: 239mg
FIBER: 8g | CARBOHYDRATES: 47g | SUGAR: 4g

Puréed Yellow Lentil Soup

This soup is simple, and allows the earthy flavor of the lentils to shine through. Inspired by a lentil soup from Egypt, this version is puréed until smooth, but you can choose to serve it chunky if you prefer. To add a little extra richness, stir in a tablespoon or two of unsalted butter just before serving.

- **Hands-On Time: 10 minutes**
- **Cook Time: 20 minutes**

Serves 6

2 tablespoons olive oil

1 stalk celery, sliced

1 medium white onion, peeled and roughly chopped

1 medium carrot, peeled and sliced

2 cloves garlic, peeled and minced

½ teaspoon ground turmeric

½ teaspoon ground cumin

½ teaspoon salt

2 cups dried yellow lentils

1 large russet potato, peeled and chopped

4 cups Beef Stock or Chicken Stock (see recipes in Chapter 2)

1 tablespoon fresh lemon juice

1 Press the Sauté button on the Instant Pot® and heat oil. Add celery, onion, and carrot and cook until just tender, about 3 minutes. Add garlic, turmeric, cumin, and salt. Cook until fragrant, about 30 seconds. Press the Cancel button.

2 Add lentils, potato, and stock to pot and stir well. Close lid, set steam release to Sealing, press the Manual button, and adjust time to 20 minutes.

3 When the timer beeps, let pressure release naturally, about 15 minutes. Remove lid and stir in lemon juice. Purée soup with an immersion blender, or in batches in a blender, until smooth. Serve warm.

PER SERVING

CALORIES: 345 | **FAT:** 8g | **PROTEIN:** 19g | **SODIUM:** 241mg
FIBER: 8g | **CARBOHYDRATES:** 51g | **SUGAR:** 3g

Red Lentil and Pumpkin Soup

Don't let the sweet spices fool you—this soup is rich, creamy, and very savory. If you have homemade pumpkin purée on hand, feel free to use it here, but reduce the cooking liquid by 1 cup. Homemade pumpkin purée is not as thick as canned, which might make the soup too thin.

- **Hands-On Time: 10 minutes**
- **Cook Time: 20 minutes**

Serves 6

2 tablespoons olive oil

2 stalks celery, sliced

1 medium yellow onion, peeled and chopped

1 medium carrot, peeled and sliced

2 cloves garlic, peeled and minced

1 teaspoon minced fresh ginger

½ teaspoon ground coriander

½ teaspoon ground turmeric

¼ teaspoon ground allspice

¼ teaspoon ground cinnamon

⅛ teaspoon ground nutmeg

½ teaspoon salt

2 cups dried red lentils

1 (15-ounce) can pumpkin purée

4 cups Roasted Vegetable Stock (see recipe in Chapter 2)

1 Press the Sauté button on the Instant Pot® and heat oil. Add celery, onion, and carrot and cook until just tender, about 3 minutes. Add garlic, ginger, coriander, turmeric, allspice, cinnamon, nutmeg, and salt. Cook until fragrant, about 30 seconds. Press the Cancel button.

2 Add lentils, pumpkin, and stock to pot and stir well. Close lid, set steam release to Sealing, press the Manual button, and adjust time to 20 minutes. When the timer beeps, let pressure release naturally, about 15 minutes. Remove lid and stir well. Serve warm.

PER SERVING

CALORIES: 341 | FAT: 9g | PROTEIN: 16g | SODIUM: 227mg
FIBER: 10g | CARBOHYDRATES: 52g | SUGAR: 6g

Black Bean and Sausage Soup

Black beans are loaded with fiber, which has been shown to help lower cholesterol. If high cholesterol is a concern for you, or if you want to reduce the fat in your diet, swap the smoked beef sausage with a leaner chicken or turkey sausage.

- **Hands-On Time: 10 minutes**
- **Cook Time: 8 minutes**

Serves 6

2 tablespoons olive oil

2 stalks celery, chopped

1 medium carrot, peeled and chopped

1 medium yellow onion, peeled and chopped

2 cloves garlic, peeled and lightly crushed

½ teaspoon salt

1 pound smoked beef sausage, cut into ½" slices

2 (15-ounce) cans black beans, drained and rinsed

½ teaspoon dried thyme leaves

¼ teaspoon dried oregano leaves

4 cups Chicken Stock (see recipe in Chapter 2)

1 Press the Sauté button on the Instant Pot® and heat oil. Add celery, carrot, and onion to pot. Cook until vegetables are tender, about 5 minutes. Add garlic and salt and cook until fragrant, about 30 seconds. Press the Cancel button.

2 Add sausage, beans, thyme, oregano, and stock to pot. Close lid and set steam release to Sealing, then press the Manual button and adjust cook time to 8 minutes.

3 When the timer beeps, let pressure release naturally, about 15–20 minutes, then open lid and stir well. Serve hot.

PER SERVING

CALORIES: 444 | FAT: 25g | PROTEIN: 22g | SODIUM: 1,395mg
FIBER: 11g | CARBOHYDRATES: 28g | SUGAR: 2g

Kidney Bean and Sausage Soup

If you can't locate bulk, or uncased, Italian sausage in your butcher's case, you can use fresh Italian sausages and remove the casings yourself. Italian sausage comes in hot and sweet varieties, and either will work here. If you are avoiding pork, you can use ground beef and a teaspoon of Italian seasoning.

- **Hands-On Time: 15 minutes**
- **Cook Time: 30 minutes**

Serves 6

½ pound bulk Italian sausage

1 large yellow onion, peeled and chopped

2 cups roughly chopped cabbage

2 cloves garlic, peeled and minced

1 teaspoon ground fennel

½ teaspoon dried oregano

1 teaspoon smoked paprika

1 pound dried kidney beans, soaked overnight in water to cover and drained

4 sprigs fresh thyme

¼ cup roughly chopped fresh flat-leaf parsley

8 cups water

½ teaspoon salt

1 Press the Sauté button on the Instant Pot® and add sausage. Cook, crumbling into ½" pieces, until sausage is browned, about 8 minutes. Add onion and cook, stirring often, until tender, about 5 minutes. Add cabbage, garlic, fennel, oregano, and paprika and cook 2 minutes until garlic and spices are fragrant.

2 Add beans, thyme, and chopped parsley to pot and toss to coat in onion and spices. Add water, then press the Cancel button. Close lid, set steam release to Sealing, press the Bean button, and cook for the default time of 30 minutes.

3 When the timer beeps, let pressure release naturally, about 15 minutes. Uncover, remove thyme sprigs, stir in salt, and serve hot.

PER SERVING

CALORIES: 404 | FAT: 12g | PROTEIN: 23g | SODIUM: 486mg
FIBER: 13g | CARBOHYDRATES: 51g | SUGAR: 3g

Heart-Healthy Black Bean Soup

Despite not having much fat, or any meat, this soup is high on flavor! The cilantro plays a critical role, adding an earthy, savory flavor.

- **Hands-On Time: 15 minutes**
- **Cook Time: 35 minutes**

Serves 6

1 tablespoon olive oil

2 stalks celery, chopped

1 medium yellow onion, peeled and chopped

2 cloves garlic, peeled and lightly crushed

½ teaspoon salt

⅓ cup chopped fresh cilantro

1 pound dried black beans, soaked overnight in water to cover and drained

½ teaspoon dried thyme leaves

½ teaspoon ground cumin

4 cups Vegetable Broth (see recipe in Chapter 2)

1 (15-ounce) can diced tomatoes with green chilies, drained

HEALTHY REFRIED BEANS
Make a tasty and healthy side dish for your next Tex-Mex meal. Strain 2 cups of beans from the soup and mash them gently with a potato masher. Cook mashed beans in a skillet over medium heat until hot, adding soup broth to keep the beans from sticking to the pan.

1 Press the Sauté button on the Instant Pot® and heat oil. Add celery and onion to pot. Cook until vegetables are tender, about 5 minutes. Add garlic and salt and cook until fragrant, about 30 seconds. Press the Cancel button.

2 Add cilantro, beans, thyme, cumin, and broth to pot. Close lid and set steam release to Sealing, then press the Bean button, and cook for the default time of 30 minutes.

3 When the timer beeps, let pressure release naturally, about 15–20 minutes, then open lid and stir in tomatoes. Press Keep Warm button and let stand for 5 minutes before serving.

PER SERVING

CALORIES: 334 | FAT: 6g | PROTEIN: 17g | SODIUM: 450mg
FIBER: 13g | CARBOHYDRATES: 56g | SUGAR: 6g

Moroccan Lentil and Sweet Potato Soup

This fragrant soup takes the better part of an afternoon to make on the stove, but with the Instant Pot® it will be ready in a fraction of the time! Leftover soup can be used for lunches and dinners through the week, and can also be frozen for up to three months.

- Hands-On Time: 10 minutes
- Cook Time: 20 minutes

Serves 6

2 tablespoons olive oil

2 stalks celery, sliced

1 medium carrot, peeled and sliced

1 medium yellow onion, peeled and roughly chopped

2 cloves garlic, peeled and minced

1 tablespoon minced fresh ginger

1 teaspoon ground cumin

½ teaspoon ground turmeric

½ teaspoon garam masala

¼ teaspoon ground cinnamon

¼ teaspoon cayenne pepper

½ teaspoon salt

2 cups dried red lentils

1 medium sweet potato, peeled and diced

1 (15-ounce) can diced tomatoes, drained

4 cups Roasted Vegetable Stock (see recipe in Chapter 2)

3 tablespoons chopped fresh cilantro

1 tablespoon lemon juice

1 Press the Sauté button on the Instant Pot® and heat oil. Add celery, carrot, and onion and cook until just tender, about 3 minutes. Add garlic, ginger, cumin, turmeric, garam masala, cinnamon, cayenne pepper, and salt. Cook until fragrant, about 30 seconds. Press the Cancel button.

2 Add lentils, sweet potato, tomatoes, and stock. Close lid, set steam release to Sealing, press the Manual button, and adjust time to 20 minutes. When the timer beeps, let pressure release naturally, about 15 minutes. Remove lid and stir in cilantro and lemon juice. Serve warm.

PER SERVING

CALORIES: 348 | FAT: 8g | PROTEIN: 17g | SODIUM: 360mg
FIBER: 10g | CARBOHYDRATES: 53g | SUGAR: 6g

Spiced Green Lentil and Coconut Milk Soup

This Thai-inspired soup uses ready-made red curry paste that is found in small jars near the soy sauce and rice noodles in the international section of most supermarkets. Curry paste marries well with the coconut milk, giving this soup a sweet and savory edge. Be sure to use full-fat coconut milk here for the best flavor and maximum richness.

- **Hands-On Time: 10 minutes**
- **Cook Time: 20 minutes**

Serves 6

2 tablespoons olive oil

2 stalks celery, sliced

1 medium white onion, peeled and chopped

2 medium carrots, peeled and sliced

2 cloves garlic, minced

1 teaspoon minced ginger

1 tablespoon Thai red curry paste

½ teaspoon ground coriander

½ teaspoon ground cumin

¼ teaspoon cayenne pepper

¼ teaspoon smoked paprika

½ teaspoon salt

2 cups dried green lentils

1 large russet potato, peeled and cubed

4 cups Roasted Vegetable Stock (see recipe in Chapter 2)

1 (13.66-ounce) can full-fat coconut milk

2 tablespoons fresh lime juice

2 tablespoons chopped fresh cilantro

½ teaspoon black pepper

1 Press the Sauté button on the Instant Pot® and heat oil. Add celery, onion, and carrots and cook until just tender, about 3 minutes. Add garlic, ginger, curry paste, coriander, cumin, cayenne pepper, paprika, and salt. Cook until fragrant, about 30 seconds. Press the Cancel button.

2 Add lentils, potato, stock, and coconut milk to pot and stir well. Close lid, set steam release to Sealing, press the Manual button, and adjust time to 20 minutes. When the timer beeps, let pressure release naturally, about 15 minutes. Remove lid and stir in lime juice. Serve warm with cilantro and black pepper for garnish.

PER SERVING

CALORIES: 305 | FAT: 19g | PROTEIN: 9g | SODIUM: 302mg
FIBER: 7g | CARBOHYDRATES: 27g | SUGAR: 4g

Bisques and Puréed Soups

Bisques and puréed soups are rich, silky, and slightly more elegant than soups of the chunky and hearty variety. Originally, a bisque was a soup made from game birds, but in the seventeenth century the term was used to describe a shellfish-based soup thickened with rice or ground seafood shells, then enriched with cream. Today most bisques are thickened with flour and then puréed and can be made with a variety of ingredients, not just seafood.

The Instant Pot® speeds up the simmering and thickening phases of bisque and puréed soup making. On the stove, you need to simmer a soup for up to 2 hours to ensure the ingredients are tender enough to be blended into a silky soup. With the Instant Pot®, that time can be cut back considerably, in some cases to as few as 5 minutes. Once simmering is complete, you purée the soup (right in the Instant Pot® if you have an immersion blender), add the cream and any delicate ingredients, and it's done!

So impress your dinner guests, or make a weeknight special, with a rich, creamy bowl of bisque or puréed soup. Only you need to know how easy it was.

Lobster Bisque

The Seafood Stock can be made using the shells from the lobster used here. If you find the bisque too thin after cooking you can simmer it for 8–10 minutes, stirring often, before adding the lobster.

- **Hands-On Time: 15 minutes**
- **Cook Time: 15 minutes**

Serves 6

¼ cup unsalted butter

4 stalks celery, finely chopped

2 large carrots, peeled and finely chopped

1 medium yellow onion, peeled and finely chopped

2 cloves garlic, peeled and minced

¼ teaspoon ground white pepper

¼ cup all-purpose flour

3 cups Seafood Stock (see recipe in Chapter 2)

1 bay leaf

2 pounds raw lobster tail meat, chopped

2 cups heavy cream

1 tablespoon dry sherry

1 Press the Sauté button on the Instant Pot® and melt butter. Once melted add celery, carrots, and onion. Cook until tender, about 5 minutes. Add garlic and pepper and cook until fragrant, about 30 seconds.

2 Sprinkle flour over vegetables and stir to combine, then cook 1 minute, making sure all flour is moistened. Slowly add 1 cup stock, scraping bottom of pot well. Whisk in remaining stock and bay leaf. Press the Cancel button.

3 Close lid and set steam release to Sealing, then press the Manual button and adjust cook time to 5 minutes.

4 When the timer beeps, let pressure release naturally, about 15 minutes. Uncover, stir well, and remove bay leaf. Use an immersion blender, or work in batches with a blender, to purée soup until smooth.

5 Add lobster, cream, and sherry to pot. Let stand on the Keep Warm setting until lobster is cooked through, about 10 minutes. Serve hot.

PER SERVING

CALORIES: 504 | FAT: 36g | PROTEIN: 29g | SODIUM: 801mg
FIBER: 2g | CARBOHYDRATES: 11g | SUGAR: 4g

Crab Bisque

Lump crabmeat can be found packed into containers in the refrigerated section of your seafood market or grocery store. This crab has a firm texture and is fully cooked and ready to eat. If you are unable to find this, you can use best-quality jumbo lump canned crab. Avoid claw meat—it tends to fall apart in the soup.

- **Hands-On Time: 15 minutes**
- **Cook Time: 15 minutes**

Serves 6

¼ cup unsalted butter

3 stalks celery, finely chopped

1 large carrot, peeled and finely chopped

1 medium yellow onion, peeled and finely chopped

½ medium red bell pepper, seeded and finely chopped

1 clove garlic, peeled and minced

¼ teaspoon seafood seasoning

¼ cup all-purpose flour

3 cups Seafood Stock (see recipe in Chapter 2)

2 sprigs fresh thyme

1 bay leaf

4 cups lump crabmeat

1½ cups heavy cream

1 tablespoon dry sherry

1 Press the Sauté button on the Instant Pot® and melt butter. Add celery, carrot, onion, and bell pepper. Cook until tender, about 5 minutes. Add garlic and seafood seasoning and cook until fragrant, about 30 seconds.

2 Sprinkle flour over vegetables and stir to combine, then cook 1 minute, making sure all flour is moistened. Slowly add 1 cup stock, scraping bottom of pot well. Whisk in remaining stock, thyme, and bay leaf. Press the Cancel button.

3 Close lid and set steam release to Sealing, then press the Manual button and adjust cook time to 5 minutes.

4 When the timer beeps, let pressure release naturally, about 15 minutes. Uncover, stir well, and remove thyme and bay leaf. Use an immersion blender, or work in batches with a blender, to purée soup until smooth.

5 Add crab, cream, and sherry to pot. Let stand on the Keep Warm setting until crab is cooked through, about 10 minutes. Serve hot.

PER SERVING

CALORIES: 462 | FAT: 36g | PROTEIN: 20g | SODIUM: 656mg
FIBER: 1g | CARBOHYDRATES: 11g | SUGAR: 5g

Tomato Bisque

Look for canned whole plum tomatoes, which retain the best balance between acidity and sweetness after canning. While not terribly authentic, butter is used in place of olive oil here. The butter adds a savory richness that makes the bisque irresistible.

- **Hands-On Time: 20 minutes**
- **Cook Time: 10 minutes**

Serves 6

½ cup unsalted butter

1 medium yellow onion, peeled and finely chopped

2 cloves garlic, peeled and minced

1 tablespoon tomato paste

1½ teaspoons ground fennel

1 teaspoon dried oregano

½ teaspoon dried thyme

¼ teaspoon crushed red pepper flakes

1 (28-ounce) can whole plum tomatoes

2 cups Chicken Stock (see recipe in Chapter 2)

1 bay leaf

2 cups heavy cream

3 tablespoons chopped fresh basil

1 Press the Sauté button on the Instant Pot® and melt butter. Add onion and cook until tender, about 5 minutes. Add garlic and tomato paste and cook until fragrant and the tomato paste is slightly darker in color, about 1 minute. Add fennel, oregano, thyme, and red pepper flakes and cook until fragrant, about 30 seconds. Press the Cancel button.

2 Add tomatoes, stock, and bay leaf and stir well. Close lid and set steam release to Sealing, then press the Manual button and adjust cook time to 5 minutes.

3 When the timer beeps, let pressure release naturally, about 15 minutes. Uncover, stir well, and remove bay leaf. Use an immersion blender, or work in batches with a blender, to purée soup until smooth.

4 Add cream to pot. Let stand on the Keep Warm setting to warm cream, about 5 minutes. Serve hot with basil for garnish.

PER SERVING

CALORIES: 464 | FAT: 43g | PROTEIN: 3g | SODIUM: 407mg
FIBER: 2g | CARBOHYDRATES: 13g | SUGAR: 10g

Sweet Corn Bisque

Nothing captures the flavor of summer better than a creamy and sweet corn soup. If you happen to be making this soup out of season, use 2 cups frozen corn kernels.

- Hands-On Time: 20 minutes
- Cook Time: 17 minutes

Serves 6

¼ cup unsalted butter

1 medium white onion, peeled and diced

2 cloves garlic, peeled and minced

4 sprigs fresh tarragon, leaves stripped and finely chopped, stems reserved

5 medium ears corn, husked

4 cups Chicken Stock (see recipe in Chapter 2)

1 bay leaf

1 cup heavy cream

½ teaspoon salt

½ teaspoon ground black pepper

3 tablespoons chopped chives

TIPS FOR SELECTING FRESH CORN

When picking corn, look for tightly wrapped, green, unblemished husks. Feel through the husk. If you can feel the kernels of corn, you know they are plump. Don't buy corn with large gaps between kernels. Finally, examine the silk. If it's dark, dry, or missing, put that ear back.

1 Press the Sauté button on the Instant Pot® and melt butter. Add onion and cook until tender, about 5 minutes. Add garlic and tarragon leaves and stems and cook until fragrant, about 30 seconds. Press the Cancel button.

2 Cut kernels from each ear of corn and cut cobs in half. Add corn, corn cobs, stock, and bay leaf and stir well. Close lid and set steam release to Sealing, then press the Manual button and adjust cook time to 12 minutes.

3 When the timer beeps, let pressure release naturally, about 15 minutes. Uncover, stir well, and remove cobs, tarragon stems, and bay leaf. Use an immersion blender, or work in batches with a blender, to purée soup until smooth.

4 Add cream, salt, and pepper to pot. Let stand on the Keep Warm setting to warm cream, about 5 minutes. Serve hot with chives for garnish.

PER SERVING

CALORIES: 300 | FAT: 23g | PROTEIN: 5g | SODIUM: 228mg
FIBER: 2g | CARBOHYDRATES: 19g | SUGAR: 7g

Curried Pumpkin Bisque

Sugar or pie pumpkins are readily available in most produce markets in the fall and winter. If you are unable to find fresh pumpkin in your local market, you can substitute a 28-ounce can of pumpkin purée. Be sure to check the label and make sure you're not buying pumpkin pie filling!

- Hands-On Time: 20 minutes
- Cook Time: 22 minutes

Serves 6

1 sugar or pie pumpkin, cut in half, stem and seeds removed

1 cup water

¼ cup unsalted butter

1 medium yellow onion, peeled and finely chopped

1 medium carrot, peeled and finely chopped

2 cloves garlic, peeled and minced

1 teaspoon garam masala

½ teaspoon ground cinnamon

½ teaspoon ground cumin

½ teaspoon ground coriander

3 cups Vegetable Broth or Chicken Stock (see recipes in Chapter 2)

2 cups heavy cream

3 tablespoons chopped fresh cilantro

1. Place pumpkin and water in the Instant Pot®. Close lid, set steam release to Sealing, press the Manual button, and adjust time to 12 minutes. When the timer beeps, let pressure release naturally, about 20 minutes. Open lid, transfer pumpkin to cutting board, and drain off liquid. Scoop out pumpkin flesh into a large bowl and set aside.

2. Return pot to machine, making sure it is wiped dry. Press the Sauté button and melt butter. Add onion and carrot and cook until tender, about 5 minutes. Add garlic, garam masala, cinnamon, cumin, and coriander and cook until fragrant and the spices are darker in color, about 1 minute. Press the Cancel button.

3. Add pumpkin and broth and stir well. Close lid and set steam release to Sealing, then press the Manual button and adjust cook time to 5 minutes.

4. When the timer beeps, let pressure release naturally, about 15 minutes. Remove lid and stir well. Use an immersion blender, or work in batches with a blender, to purée soup until smooth.

5. Add cream to pot. Let stand on the Keep Warm setting to warm cream, about 5 minutes. Serve hot with cilantro for garnish.

PER SERVING

CALORIES: 477 | FAT: 36g | PROTEIN: 6g | SODIUM: 45mg
FIBER: 3g | CARBOHYDRATES: 34g | SUGAR: 15g

Butternut Squash Soup

This soup makes an elegant beginning to a holiday dinner, or a comforting yet sophisticated lunch on a cold day. The dash of maple syrup added to the soup enriches the natural sweetness of the butternut squash, but you can leave it out if you prefer.

- **Hands-On Time: 20 minutes**
- **Cook Time: 20 minutes**

Serves 6

¼ **cup unsalted butter**

1 **medium yellow onion, peeled and finely chopped**

1 **medium carrot, peeled and finely chopped**

2 **cloves garlic, peeled and minced**

3 **cups cubed butternut squash**

½ **teaspoon dried thyme**

¼ **teaspoon ground cinnamon**

¼ **teaspoon ground cumin**

3 **cups Vegetable Broth or Chicken Stock (see recipes in Chapter 2)**

2 **tablespoons maple syrup**

1 **cup heavy cream**

¼ **cup sour cream**

3 **tablespoons chopped fresh chives**

1 Press the Sauté button on the Instant Pot® and melt butter. Add onion and carrot and cook until tender, about 5 minutes. Add garlic, squash, thyme, cinnamon, and cumin and cook until fragrant, about 1 minute. Press the Cancel button.

2 Add stock and maple syrup and stir well. Close lid and set steam release to Sealing, then press the Manual button and adjust cook time to 15 minutes.

3 When the timer beeps, let pressure release naturally, about 15 minutes. Remove lid and stir well. Use an immersion blender, or work in batches with a blender, to purée soup until smooth.

4 Mix cream and sour cream in a small bowl, then stir into soup. Let stand on the Keep Warm setting to warm cream, about 5 minutes. Serve hot with chives for garnish.

PER SERVING

CALORIES: 295 | FAT: 24g | PROTEIN: 2g | SODIUM: 33mg
FIBER: 2g | CARBOHYDRATES: 18g | SUGAR: 8g

Green Pea and Mint Bisque

Peas and mint are a match made in heaven, and this soup lets the flavor dream team shine. It's perfect with roast lamb, which is often served with mushy peas and mint jelly, or served alone with crisp croutons on top for a crunchy garnish.

- **Hands-On Time: 20 minutes**
- **Cook Time: 10 minutes**

Serves 6

¼ cup unsalted butter

1 stalk celery, finely chopped

1 medium leek, white and light green parts only, finely chopped

1 clove garlic, peeled and minced

1 tablespoon minced fresh mint leaves

½ teaspoon dried thyme

⅛ teaspoon ground nutmeg

3 cups Vegetable Broth or Chicken Stock (see recipes in Chapter 2)

1 pound frozen green peas

½ cup heavy cream

ENVIRONMENTAL BENEFITS OF GREEN PEAS

Green peas are "nitrogen-fixing" plants—they take nitrogen from the air and transform it into a form that can help replenish the soil without added fertilizers. They also have shorter root structure, so they don't cause soil erosion and they require less water.

1 Press the Sauté button on the Instant Pot® and melt butter. Add celery and leek and cook until tender, about 5 minutes. Add garlic, mint, thyme, and nutmeg and cook until fragrant, about 1 minute. Press the Cancel button.

2 Add broth and peas and stir well. Close lid and set steam release to Sealing, then press the Manual button and adjust cook time to 5 minutes.

3 When the timer beeps, let pressure release naturally, about 15 minutes. Remove lid and stir well. Use an immersion blender, or work in batches with a blender, to purée soup until smooth.

4 Add cream to pot and mix well. Let stand on the Keep Warm setting to warm cream, about 5 minutes. Serve hot.

PER SERVING

CALORIES: 215 | FAT: 15g | PROTEIN: 5g | SODIUM: 100mg
FIBER: 4g | CARBOHYDRATES: 14g | SUGAR: 5g

Creamy Mushroom Bisque

Browning the mushrooms in batches may take a little longer, but it ensures you get the most complex, rich flavor and even browning. If you choose, you can totally skip this step and still have amazing results.

- **Hands-On Time: 20 minutes**
- **Cook Time: 5 minutes**

Serves 6

1 (½-ounce) bag dried wild mushrooms

2 cups boiling water

3 tablespoons unsalted butter, divided

4 cups sliced cremini mushrooms, divided

2 stalks celery, chopped

1 medium onion, peeled and chopped

2 cloves garlic, peeled and minced

½ teaspoon dried thyme

1 bay leaf

2 cups Chicken Broth or Vegetable Broth (see recipes in Chapter 2)

½ cup heavy cream

1 In a medium heatproof bowl add dried mushrooms and boiling water. Let stand until fully rehydrated, about 30 minutes. Strain mushrooms and reserve soaking liquid.

2 Press the Sauté button on the Instant Pot® and melt 1 tablespoon butter. Add 2 cups cremini mushrooms and let stand without stirring for 3 minutes, or until golden. Stir well, then remove from pot. Melt another tablespoon butter and brown the remaining 2 cups cremini mushrooms for 3 minutes. Remove from pot.

3 Add remaining 1 tablespoon butter to the pot. Sauté celery and onion until tender, about 4–5 minutes, then add garlic and thyme and cook until fragrant, about 1 minute. Press the Cancel button and add soaked mushrooms, 1 cup reserved soaking liquid, browned cremini mushrooms, bay leaf, and broth. Stir well.

4 Close lid, set steam release to Sealing, press the Manual button, and set time to 5 minutes. When the timer beeps, quick-release the pressure. Press the Cancel button, open lid, and discard bay leaf. Stir well, then purée soup with an immersion blender or in batches in a blender. Stir in cream. Serve hot.

PER SERVING

CALORIES: 146 | FAT: 12g | PROTEIN: 3g | SODIUM: 330mg
FIBER: 1g | CARBOHYDRATES: 6g | SUGAR: 3g

Cauliflower Bisque

Cauliflower is versatile, flavorful, and nutritious. It is also a good source of fiber, so eating cauliflower will help you feel fuller longer. If you are feeling adventurous, try making this soup with orange or purple cauliflower.

- **Hands-On Time: 15 minutes**
- **Cook Time: 20 minutes**

Serves 6

4 tablespoons unsalted butter

1 medium yellow onion, peeled and chopped

1 stalk celery, chopped

1 medium carrot, peeled and chopped

½ teaspoon dried thyme

4 cups fresh cauliflower florets

2 cups Chicken Stock (see recipe in Chapter 2)

2 cups heavy cream

⅓ cup chopped fresh chives

1 Press the Sauté button on the Instant Pot® and melt butter. Add onion, celery, and carrot. Cook, stirring often, 3 minutes. Add thyme, cauliflower, and stock. Stir well, then press the Cancel button.

2 Close lid and set steam release to Sealing, then press the Manual button and adjust cook time to 8 minutes.

3 When the timer beeps, let pressure release naturally, about 15 minutes. Remove lid and use an immersion blender, or work in batches in a blender, to purée soup until smooth.

4 Stir in cream and chives, then let soup stand on the Keep Warm setting for 5 minutes to warm cream. Serve hot.

PER SERVING

CALORIES: 379 | FAT: 35g | PROTEIN: 4g | SODIUM: 68mg
FIBER: 2g | CARBOHYDRATES: 9g | SUGAR: 5g

Puréed Fennel and Carrot Soup

Most people associate fennel with the seeds, which are used commonly in sausage. Fresh fennel bulb has a subtle anise flavor with a bright, almost onion-like flavor at the finish. It can be shaved and served raw in salads, or chopped and cooked in soups, stews, and roasts.

- **Hands-On Time: 20 minutes**
- **Cook Time: 20 minutes**

Serves 6

¼ cup unsalted butter

2 medium carrots, peeled and finely chopped

1 medium fennel bulb, trimmed and chopped

1 medium yellow onion, peeled and finely chopped

1 clove garlic, peeled and minced

1 teaspoon dried dill

½ teaspoon dried thyme

3 cups Vegetable Broth or Chicken Stock (see recipes in Chapter 2)

½ cup heavy cream

3 tablespoons chopped dill fronds

HOW TO PREPARE A FRESH FENNEL BULB

First, trim off the stalks, but be sure to reserve the fronds for adding to other dishes as they have a lot of flavor. Wash the bulb well, then slice in half and then into quarters. Peel away any brown or damaged layers. Next, slice, shave, or chop the fennel as needed.

1 Press the Sauté button on the Instant Pot® and melt butter. Add carrots, fennel, and onion and cook until tender, about 5 minutes. Add garlic, dill, and thyme and cook until fragrant, about 1 minute. Press the Cancel button.

2 Add broth and stir well. Close lid and set steam release to Sealing, then press the Manual button and adjust cook time to 10 minutes.

3 When the timer beeps, let pressure release naturally, about 15 minutes. Remove lid and stir well. Use an immersion blender, or work in batches with a blender, to purée soup until smooth.

4 Add cream to pot and mix well. Let stand on the Keep Warm setting to warm cream, about 5 minutes. Serve hot with dill for garnish.

PER SERVING

CALORIES: 174 | **FAT:** 15g | **PROTEIN:** 1g | **SODIUM:** 45mg
FIBER: 2g | **CARBOHYDRATES:** 8g | **SUGAR:** 4g

Roasted Red Pepper Bisque

Jarred roasted red bell peppers are a fantastic shortcut that will save you time and mess in the kitchen. They are typically available in the grocery store near the olives.

- **Hands-On Time: 20 minutes**
- **Cook Time: 15 minutes**

Serves 6

½ cup unsalted butter

1 medium yellow onion, peeled and diced

1 medium carrot, peeled and diced

2 cloves garlic, peeled and minced

1 teaspoon dried oregano

½ teaspoon dried thyme

¼ teaspoon crushed red pepper flakes

1 (16-ounce) jar roasted red peppers, roughly chopped

2 cups Chicken Stock (see recipe in Chapter 2)

1 bay leaf

2 cups heavy cream

GRUYÈRE AND CHEDDAR GRILLED CHEESE

Generously butter two slices of bread and place in a skillet, butter side down, over medium-low heat. Add a handful of grated Gruyère and smoked Cheddar to each slice. Cover and cook 1 minute. Uncover, place one slice of bread on the other and continue to toast, flipping often, until the bread is golden brown and the cheese is oozing. Slice and serve.

1 Press the Sauté button on the Instant Pot® and melt butter. Add onion and carrot and cook until tender, about 5 minutes. Add garlic and cook until fragrant, about 30 seconds. Add oregano, thyme, and red pepper flakes and cook until fragrant, about 30 seconds. Press the Cancel button.

2 Add roasted red peppers, stock, and bay leaf and stir well. Close lid and set steam release to Sealing, then press the Manual button and adjust cook time to 5 minutes.

3 When the timer beeps, let pressure release naturally, about 15 minutes. Uncover, stir well, and remove bay leaf. Use an immersion blender, or work in batches with a blender, to purée soup until smooth.

4 Add cream to pot. Let stand on the Keep Warm setting to warm cream, about 5 minutes. Serve hot.

PER SERVING

CALORIES: 441 | **FAT:** 42g | **PROTEIN:** 3g | **SODIUM:** 317mg
FIBER: 1g | **CARBOHYDRATES:** 8g | **SUGAR:** 6g

Shrimp Bisque

Unless you live near the coast, you will probably have a difficult time finding shrimp that have not been previously frozen. However, most shrimp are processed and frozen within minutes of being caught, so their freshness is preserved.

- **Hands-On Time: 20 minutes**
- **Cook Time: 15 minutes**

Serves 6

¼ cup unsalted butter

2 stalks celery, finely chopped

2 large carrots, peeled and finely chopped

2 medium leeks, white and light green parts chopped

2 cloves garlic, peeled and minced

½ teaspoon seafood seasoning

¼ cup all-purpose flour

3 cups Seafood Stock (see recipe in Chapter 2)

1 bay leaf

2 pounds raw peeled and deveined shrimp, chopped

2 cups heavy cream

1 tablespoon dry sherry

1 teaspoon ground black pepper

1 Press the Sauté button on the Instant Pot® and melt butter. Add celery, carrots, and leeks. Cook until tender, about 5 minutes. Add garlic and seafood seasoning and cook until fragrant, about 30 seconds.

2 Sprinkle flour over vegetables and stir to combine, then cook 1 minute, making sure all flour is moistened. Slowly add 1 cup stock, scraping bottom of pot well. Whisk in remaining stock and bay leaf. Press the Cancel button.

3 Close lid and set steam release to Sealing, then press the Manual button and adjust cook time to 5 minutes.

4 When the timer beeps, let pressure release naturally, about 15 minutes. Uncover, stir well, and remove bay leaf. Use an immersion blender, or work in batches with a blender, to purée soup until smooth.

5 Add shrimp, cream, and sherry to pot. Let stand on the Keep Warm setting until shrimp is cooked through, about 10 minutes. Sprinkle with pepper and serve hot.

PER SERVING

CALORIES: 505 | FAT: 36g | PROTEIN: 25g | SODIUM: 1,011mg
FIBER: 2g | CARBOHYDRATES: 15g | SUGAR: 5g

Squash and Cheese Soup

Emmental cheese is a Swiss cheese most commonly used in fondue as it melts exceptionally well. It has a mild, nutty, and savory flavor. In creamy, lightly sweet butternut squash bisque, Emmental is paired with a little sharp Cheddar for a bit of a bite.

- **Hands-On Time: 15 minutes**
- **Cook Time: 20 minutes**

Serves 6

¼ cup unsalted butter

1 medium yellow onion, peeled and finely chopped

1 medium carrot, peeled and finely chopped

2 cloves garlic, peeled and minced

¼ cup white wine

½ teaspoon dried thyme

⅛ teaspoon ground nutmeg

3 cups cubed butternut squash

2 cups Vegetable Broth or Chicken Stock (see recipes in Chapter 2)

2 tablespoons maple syrup

2 cups heavy cream

1 cup grated Emmental cheese

½ cup grated sharp Cheddar cheese

3 tablespoons chopped fresh chives

1 Press the Sauté button on the Instant Pot® and melt butter. Add onion and carrot and cook until tender, about 5 minutes. Add garlic and cook until fragrant, about 30 seconds. Add wine and cook, scraping pot well, until mostly evaporated, about 30 seconds. Press the Cancel button.

2 Add thyme, nutmeg, squash, and broth to pot and stir well. Close lid and set steam release to Sealing, then press the Manual button and adjust cook time to 15 minutes.

3 When the timer beeps, let pressure release naturally, about 15 minutes. Remove lid and stir in maple syrup. Use an immersion blender, or work in batches with a blender, to purée soup until smooth.

4 Stir cream into soup, then whisk in both grated cheeses ¼ cup at a time, adding more cheese once the previous addition is fully melted. Let stand on the Keep Warm setting for 5 minutes. Serve hot with chives for garnish.

PER SERVING

CALORIES: 520 | **FAT:** 43g | **PROTEIN:** 10g | **SODIUM:** 116mg
FIBER: 2g | **CARBOHYDRATES:** 20g | **SUGAR:** 9g

Carrot Apple Soup

Tart Granny Smith apples give this soup a refreshing edge that plays well with the natural sweetness of the carrots and cream. If you prefer a less tart apple, stick to varieties that are firmer, such as Pink Lady or Fuji, to keep the deep apple flavor without adding too much sweetness.

- **Hands-On Time: 20 minutes**
- **Cook Time: 15 minutes**

Serves 6

¼ cup unsalted butter

4 medium carrots, peeled and finely chopped

2 medium Granny Smith apples, cored and chopped

½ medium sweet onion, peeled and finely chopped

1 clove garlic, peeled and minced

1 teaspoon grated fresh ginger

½ teaspoon dried tarragon

⅛ teaspoon ground nutmeg

3 cups Vegetable Broth or Chicken Stock (see recipes in Chapter 2)

¾ cup heavy cream

½ teaspoon salt

½ teaspoon ground black pepper

3 tablespoons chopped fresh chives

1 Press the Sauté button on the Instant Pot® and melt butter. Add carrots and cook until tender, about 5 minutes. Add apples, onion, garlic, ginger, tarragon, and nutmeg and cook until fragrant, about 2 minutes. Press the Cancel button.

2 Add broth and stir well. Close lid and set steam release to Sealing, then press the Manual button and adjust cook time to 10 minutes.

3 When the timer beeps, let pressure release naturally, about 15 minutes. Remove lid and stir well. Use an immersion blender, or work in batches with a blender, to purée soup until smooth. Stir in cream, salt, and pepper. Sprinkle with chives and serve hot.

PER SERVING

CALORIES: 227 | FAT: 19g | PROTEIN: 1g | SODIUM: 236mg
FIBER: 2g | CARBOHYDRATES: 13g | SUGAR: 9g

Puréed Cauliflower and Roasted Garlic Soup

If you are watching your carbohydrate intake but want a creamy bowl of soup, this may be the answer you are looking for! Cauliflower is naturally low in carbs, but can stand in for potatoes quite well! If you have roasted or puréed cauliflower on hand, you can use it in this soup; just reduce the volume to 3 cups.

- **Hands-On Time: 15 minutes**
- **Cook Time: 10 minutes**

Serves 6

4 tablespoons olive oil

2 medium leeks, white and light green parts only, finely chopped

1 stalk celery, chopped

1 medium carrot, peeled and chopped

½ teaspoon dried thyme

⅛ teaspoon ground nutmeg

6 cloves roasted garlic, peeled and mashed into paste

4 cups fresh cauliflower florets

4 cups Chicken Stock (see recipe in Chapter 2)

3 tablespoons chopped fresh flat-leaf parsley

1 Press the Sauté button on the Instant Pot® and heat olive oil. Add leeks, celery, and carrot. Cook, stirring often, 3 minutes. Add thyme and nutmeg and cook until fragrant, about 30 seconds. Press the Cancel button, then stir in roasted garlic.

2 Add cauliflower and stock and stir well. Close lid and set steam release to Sealing, then press the Manual button and adjust cook time to 10 minutes.

3 When the timer beeps, let pressure release naturally, about 15 minutes. Remove lid and use an immersion blender, or work in batches in a blender, to purée soup until smooth. Serve hot with parsley for garnish.

PER SERVING

CALORIES: 139 | FAT: 10g | PROTEIN: 4g | SODIUM: 46mg
FIBER: 3g | CARBOHYDRATES: 10g | SUGAR: 3g

Vegan Root Vegetable Bisque

If you want to deepen the flavor of this bisque, you can roast the onion, parsnip, celery root, and carrot beforehand. Set your oven to 375°F, coat vegetables in olive oil, and roast for 30–40 minutes, or until tender. Skip the sauté step, and just load everything except the parsley into the pot and proceed as directed.

- **Hands-On Time: 25 minutes**
- **Cook Time: 12 minutes**

Serves 6

4 tablespoons olive oil

1 medium onion, peeled and finely chopped

1 medium parsnip, peeled and finely chopped

1 medium celery root or celeriac, peeled and finely chopped

1 medium carrot, peeled and chopped

2 cloves garlic, peeled and minced

½ teaspoon dried thyme

½ teaspoon smoked paprika

1 cup peeled, seeded, and cubed butternut squash

1 small russet potato, peeled and cubed

6 cups Roasted Vegetable Stock (see recipe in Chapter 2)

3 tablespoons chopped fresh flat-leaf parsley

1 Press the Sauté button on the Instant Pot® and heat olive oil. Add onion, parsnip, celery root, and carrot. Cook, stirring often, until tender, about 12 minutes. Add garlic, thyme and paprika and cook until fragrant, about 30 seconds. Press the Cancel button.

2 Add squash, potato, and stock and stir well. Close lid and set steam release to Sealing, then press the Manual button and adjust cook time to 12 minutes.

3 When the timer beeps, let pressure release naturally, about 15 minutes. Remove lid and use an immersion blender, or work in batches in a blender, to purée soup until smooth. Serve hot with parsley for garnish.

PER SERVING

CALORIES: 197 | FAT: 11g | PROTEIN: 3g | SODIUM: 97mg
FIBER: 4g | CARBOHYDRATES: 24g | SUGAR: 6g

Vegan Spiced Sweet Potato Soup

This creamy soup mixes warm spices like cumin and smoked paprika with sweet spices like allspice and cinnamon to make a delectable dish. If you have leftover roasted sweet potatoes, you can use them in place of all or part of the raw sweet potatoes.

- **Hands-On Time: 15 minutes**
- **Cook Time: 8 minutes**

Serves 6

4 tablespoons olive oil

1 large leek, white and light green parts only, finely chopped

2 cloves garlic, peeled and minced

½ teaspoon ground cumin

¼ teaspoon smoked paprika

¼ teaspoon ground allspice

¼ teaspoon ground cinnamon

2 pounds sweet potatoes, peeled and chopped

6 cups Vegetable Broth (see recipe in Chapter 2)

¼ cup thinly sliced green scallions

½ teaspoon salt

½ teaspoon ground black pepper

1 Press the Sauté button on the Instant Pot® and heat olive oil. Add leek and garlic. Cook, stirring often, until tender, about 3 minutes. Add cumin, paprika, allspice, and cinnamon. Cook until fragrant, about 30 seconds. Press the Cancel button.

2 Add sweet potatoes and broth and stir well. Close lid and set steam release to Sealing, then press the Manual button and adjust cook time to 8 minutes.

3 When the timer beeps, let pressure release naturally, about 15 minutes. Remove lid and use an immersion blender, or work in batches in a blender, to purée soup until smooth. Stir in scallions, salt, and pepper. Serve hot.

PER SERVING

CALORIES: 234 | FAT: 11g | PROTEIN: 3g | SODIUM: 280mg
FIBER: 5g | CARBOHYDRATES: 33g | SUGAR: 7g

Carrot Bisque with Ginger and Maple

This bisque is rich in flavor, but lighter than most bisque-style soups since it has only ½ cup of cream mixed in at the end. It tastes fantastic with a grilled cheese sandwich made with sharp Cheddar and Gruyère cheeses, or alongside a peppery green salad with a sweet ginger-based dressing.

- **Hands-On Time: 20 minutes**
- **Cook Time: 15 minutes**

Serves 6

¼ cup unsalted butter

4 medium carrots, peeled and finely chopped

1 medium yellow onion, peeled and finely chopped

1 clove garlic, peeled and minced

1 tablespoon grated ginger

1 small sweet potato, peeled and diced

½ teaspoon dried thyme

¼ teaspoon ground allspice

3 cups Vegetable Broth or Chicken Stock (see recipes in Chapter 2)

¼ cup maple syrup

¾ cup heavy cream, divided

3 tablespoons chopped fresh flat-leaf parsley

1 Press the Sauté button on the Instant Pot® and melt butter. Add carrots and onion and cook until tender, about 5 minutes. Add garlic, ginger, sweet potato, thyme, and allspice and cook until fragrant, about 1 minute. Press the Cancel button.

2 Add broth and maple syrup and stir well. Close lid and set steam release to Sealing, then press the Manual button and adjust cook time to 10 minutes.

3 When the timer beeps, let pressure release naturally, about 15 minutes. Remove lid and stir well. Use an immersion blender, or work in batches with a blender, to purée soup until smooth.

4 Add ½ cup cream to pot and mix well. Let stand on the Keep Warm setting to warm cream, about 5 minutes. Serve hot with parsley and a drizzle of cream for garnish.

PER SERVING

CALORIES: 249 | **FAT:** 19g | **PROTEIN:** 2g | **SODIUM:** 48mg
FIBER: 2g | **CARBOHYDRATES:** 18g | **SUGAR:** 12g

7

Chowder and Gumbo

You may not think of gumbo and chowder as being similar, but they have a lot in common. Both are varieties of stew with origins in different parts of the world. Gumbo is synonymous with Louisiana, but the dish is a melting pot of culinary traditions, including West African, French, Caribbean, and Native American. Chowder, on the other hand, has a slightly murkier origin. It may have been brought to New England by French, English, or French Canadian settlers. Chowders can be creamy or broth based, enriched with cream or tomato, and made with all sorts of ingredients from clams and fish to corn and peppers.

Chowder isn't necessarily a long-cooking dish, but it can be a little tedious, requiring you to monitor the dish at different steps in the process. The Instant Pot® requires you to do just a few minutes of work, then you can let it do the rest. A traditional gumbo can take as many as 4 hours to make on the stove, but that time is slashed to under an hour with the Instant Pot®.

Chowders and gumbos make hearty meals, and with the Instant Pot® you don't have to wait for the weekend to make a pot of something special.

Vegetable Chowder

This vegetable-packed chowder is a meat- and seafood-free alternative to other chowders that is filling and satisfying. This recipe is a great place to use up leftover bits of vegetables from the refrigerator, or to use vegetables from a Community Supported Agriculture (CSA) or produce share box. The more vegetables the better!

- **Hands-On Time: 15 minutes**
- **Cook Time: 5 minutes**

Serves 8

4 tablespoons unsalted butter

2 stalks celery, chopped

2 medium carrots, peeled and chopped

1 medium yellow onion, peeled and diced

2 cloves garlic, peeled and minced

½ teaspoon ground black pepper

¼ teaspoon dried thyme

¼ teaspoon dried marjoram

⅓ cup all-purpose flour

4 cups Vegetable Broth (see recipe in Chapter 2)

1 bay leaf

1 pound new potatoes, diced

2 cups fresh broccoli florets

1 cup fresh cauliflower florets

2 cups heavy cream

⅓ cup chopped fresh chives

1 Press the Sauté button on the Instant Pot® and melt butter. Add celery, carrots, and onion and cook until tender, about 5 minutes. Add garlic, pepper, thyme, and marjoram and cook until fragrant, about 30 seconds.

2 Sprinkle flour over vegetables and mix well, then cook 1 minute until no dry flour remains. Slowly add broth, whisking constantly until smooth, then add bay leaf, potatoes, broccoli, and cauliflower. Press the Cancel button.

3 Close lid and set steam release to Sealing, then press the Manual button and adjust cook time to 5 minutes.

4 When the timer beeps, let pressure release naturally, about 15 minutes. Open lid and stir in cream. Discard bay leaf and serve immediately with chives for garnish.

PER SERVING

CALORIES: 346 | FAT: 27g | PROTEIN: 4g | SODIUM: 58mg
FIBER: 3g | CARBOHYDRATES: 20g | SUGAR: 4g

Fish Chowder

There are a number of different types of fish available that you can use for chowder, so you have options! Instead of haddock, try cod, catfish, grouper, or pollack. When shopping for whitefish, you want to select the freshest fish available at your fish market.

- **Hands-On Time: 15 minutes**
- **Cook Time: 6 minutes**

Serves 8

4 tablespoons unsalted butter

2 stalks celery, chopped

1 medium yellow onion, peeled and diced

2 cloves garlic, peeled and minced

½ teaspoon seafood seasoning

½ teaspoon ground black pepper

1 pound russet potatoes, peeled and diced

4 cups Fish Stock (see recipe in Chapter 2)

1 (28-ounce) can crushed tomatoes

1 bay leaf

2 pounds haddock filets, cut into ½" pieces

1. Press the Sauté button on the Instant Pot® and melt butter. Add celery and onion and cook until tender, about 8 minutes. Add garlic, seafood seasoning, and pepper and cook until fragrant, about 30 seconds.

2. Add potatoes, stock, tomatoes, and bay leaf. Stir well, then press the Cancel button.

3. Close lid and set steam release to Sealing, then press the Manual button and adjust cook time to 5 minutes.

4. When the timer beeps, quick-release the pressure. Open lid and stir in fish, then press the Cancel button. Close lid and set steam release to Sealing, then press the Manual button and adjust cook time to 0 minutes.

5. When the timer beeps, quick-release the pressure, open lid, and discard bay leaf. Serve immediately.

PER SERVING

CALORIES: 223 | FAT: 6g | PROTEIN: 23g | SODIUM: 438mg
FIBER: 3g | CARBOHYDRATES: 19g | SUGAR: 5g

Crab and Bacon Chowder

The smoky flavor of bacon combined with the naturally sweet flavor of crab is an addictive combination. When cooking bacon for soup and chowder it is best to not cook the bacon too crisp, but to cook it until it is just starting to brown. Overcooked bacon can be unpleasantly chewy in the finished soup. Feel free to chop the bacon to your preferred size. Bigger pieces are great for texture, and smaller pieces are good for a more consistent texture.

- **Hands-On Time: 20 minutes**
- **Cook Time: 15 minutes**

Serves 8

6 slices thick-cut bacon, chopped

2 stalks celery, chopped

1 medium red bell pepper, seeded and chopped

1 medium yellow onion, peeled and diced

1 small jalapeño pepper, seeded and minced

2 cloves garlic, peeled and minced

1 teaspoon seafood seasoning

½ teaspoon ground black pepper

¼ teaspoon dried thyme

⅓ cup all-purpose flour

4 cups Seafood Stock (see recipe in Chapter 2)

1 bay leaf

1 tablespoon sherry

12 ounces lump crabmeat

2 cups heavy cream

⅓ cup chopped fresh chives

1 Press the Sauté button on the Instant Pot® and add bacon. Cook until starting to crisp, about 6 minutes. Add celery, bell pepper, and onion and cook until tender, about 5 minutes. Add jalapeño, garlic, seafood seasoning, black pepper, and thyme and cook until fragrant, about 30 seconds.

2 Sprinkle flour over vegetables and mix well, then cook 1 minute until no dry flour remains. Slowly add stock, whisking constantly until smooth, then add bay leaf. Press the Cancel button.

3 Close lid and set steam release to Sealing, then press the Manual button and adjust cook time to 5 minutes.

4 When the timer beeps, let pressure release naturally, about 15 minutes. Open lid and stir in sherry, crab, and cream. Let chowder sit on the Keep Warm setting for 10 minutes. Discard bay leaf and serve immediately with chives for garnish.

PER SERVING

CALORIES: 396 | FAT: 32g | PROTEIN: 14g | SODIUM: 549mg
FIBER: 1g | CARBOHYDRATES: 9g | SUGAR: 3g

New England Clam Chowder

There is some debate as to who brought the creamy version of clam chowder to New England, but there is no debate about its popularity. It is a classic from coast to coast. If you want to make your chowder meal extra special, you can buy sourdough boule from the bakery, cut off the top of the loaf, hollow out the base, and use that as a soup bowl.

- **Hands-On Time: 15 minutes**
- **Cook Time: 5 minutes**

Serves 8

6 tablespoons unsalted butter

1 stalk celery, chopped

1 medium carrot, peeled and chopped

1 medium yellow onion, peeled and diced

2 cloves garlic, peeled and minced

½ teaspoon ground white pepper

¼ teaspoon dried thyme

¼ teaspoon dried oregano

⅓ cup all-purpose flour

4 cups Seafood Stock (see recipe in Chapter 2)

1 bay leaf

1 pound russet potatoes, peeled and diced

2 (6.5-ounce) cans chopped clams

2 cups heavy cream

⅓ cup chopped fresh chives

1 Press the Sauté button on the Instant Pot® and melt butter. Add celery, carrot, and onion and cook until tender, about 5 minutes. Add garlic, pepper, thyme, and oregano and cook until fragrant, about 30 seconds.

2 Sprinkle flour over vegetables and mix well, then cook 1 minute until no dry flour remains. Slowly add stock, whisking constantly until smooth, then add bay leaf and potatoes. Press the Cancel button.

3 Close lid and set steam release to Sealing, then press the Manual button and adjust cook time to 5 minutes.

4 When the timer beeps, let pressure release naturally, about 15 minutes. Open lid and stir in clams and cream. Discard bay leaf and serve immediately with chives for garnish.

PER SERVING

CALORIES: 419 | FAT: 39g | PROTEIN: 15g | SODIUM: 166mg
FIBER: 1g | CARBOHYDRATES: 19g | SUGAR: 2g

Manhattan Clam Chowder

Manhattan Clam Chowder has a tomato-based broth rather than the creamy broth of traditional New England chowders. The addition of tomato is thought to be due to Portuguese influence, and while the name says Manhattan, this chowder actually originates from the state of Rhode Island.

- **Hands-On Time: 20 minutes**
- **Cook Time: 5 minutes**

Serves 8

2 tablespoons unsalted butter

2 slices bacon, chopped

2 stalks celery, chopped

1 medium yellow onion, peeled and diced

2 cloves garlic, peeled and minced

½ teaspoon seafood seasoning

½ teaspoon ground black pepper

1 pound russet potatoes, peeled and diced

4 cups Seafood Stock (see recipe in Chapter 2)

1 (28-ounce) can diced tomatoes

1 bay leaf

3 (6.5-ounce) cans chopped clams

1 Press the Sauté button on the Instant Pot® and melt butter. Add bacon and cook until cooked through but not crisp, about 4 minutes. Add celery and onion and cook until tender, about 8 minutes. Add garlic, seafood seasoning, and pepper and cook until fragrant, about 30 seconds.

2 Add potatoes, stock, tomatoes, and bay leaf. Stir well, then press the Cancel button.

3 Close lid and set steam release to Sealing, then press the Manual button and adjust cook time to 5 minutes.

4 When the timer beeps, let pressure release naturally, about 15 minutes. Open lid and stir in clams. Discard bay leaf and serve immediately.

PER SERVING

CALORIES: 233 | FAT: 6g | PROTEIN: 21g | SODIUM: 395mg
FIBER: 3g | CARBOHYDRATES: 21g | SUGAR: 4g

Minorcan Clam Chowder

This chowder originates from Florida, and while it may look a lot like Manhattan-style chowder, there is a very tasty difference. The secret to this spicy chowder is the datil chili, a chili native to the area around St. Augustine, Florida. They can be tricky to source, so you can substitute habanero peppers, which have a similar flavor and punchy heat.

- **Hands-On Time: 15 minutes**
- **Cook Time: 15 minutes**

Serves 8

2 tablespoons unsalted butter

2 ounces salt pork, finely chopped

1 medium green bell pepper, seeded and chopped

1 medium yellow onion, peeled and diced

2 cloves garlic, peeled and minced

1 datil chili, seeded and minced

3 medium tomatoes, seeded and chopped

1 teaspoon dried basil

1 teaspoon dried thyme

½ teaspoon dried marjoram

¼ teaspoon dried oregano

½ teaspoon ground black pepper

1 pound new potatoes, diced

1 (28-ounce) can crushed tomatoes

1 bay leaf

3 cups Fish Stock (see recipe in Chapter 2)

1 cup clam juice

2 (6.5-ounce) cans chopped clams

1 Press the Sauté button on the Instant Pot® and melt butter. Add salt pork and cook until fat has rendered and pork is crisp, about 3 minutes. Add bell pepper and onion and cook until tender, about 5 minutes. Add garlic, chili, tomatoes, basil, thyme, marjoram, oregano, and black pepper and cook until fragrant, about 30 seconds. Press the Cancel button.

2 Add potatoes, crushed tomatoes, bay leaf, stock, and clam juice. Close lid and set steam release to Sealing, then press the Manual button and adjust cook time to 10 minutes.

3 When the timer beeps, quick-release the pressure. Open lid and discard bay leaf. Stir in clams and let stand on the Keep Warm setting for 5 minutes. Serve hot.

PER SERVING

CALORIES: 250 | FAT: 9g | PROTEIN: 16g | SODIUM: 542mg
FIBER: 5g | CARBOHYDRATES: 26g | SUGAR: 8g

Gluten-Free Clam Chowder

Chowder is traditionally thickened with all-purpose flour, so people on a gluten-free diet often have to pass. Here the flour is removed and a cornstarch slurry is used to thicken the chowder at the end of cooking. If you prefer you can use the same amount of potato starch if you have it on hand.

- **Hands-On Time: 20 minutes**
- **Cook Time: 7 minutes**

Serves 8

6 tablespoons unsalted butter

1 stalk celery, chopped

1 medium carrot, peeled and chopped

1 medium yellow onion, peeled and diced

2 cloves garlic, peeled and minced

½ teaspoon ground white pepper

½ teaspoon dried thyme

¼ teaspoon dried oregano

4 cups Seafood Stock (see recipe in Chapter 2), divided

1 bay leaf

1 pound russet potatoes, peeled and diced

3 tablespoons cornstarch

2 (6.5-ounce) cans chopped clams

2 cups heavy cream

½ teaspoon salt

⅓ cup chopped fresh chives

1 Press the Sauté button on the Instant Pot® and melt butter. Add celery, carrot, and onion and cook until tender, about 5 minutes. Add garlic, pepper, thyme, and oregano and cook until fragrant, about 30 seconds.

2 Add 3 cups stock, bay leaf and potatoes. Press the Cancel button. Close lid and set steam release to Sealing, then press the Manual button and adjust cook time to 5 minutes.

3 When the timer beeps, let pressure release naturally, about 15 minutes. Open lid and stir well. Press the Cancel button, then press the Sauté button. Whisk reserved stock with cornstarch, then whisk into pot. Simmer until chowder thickens, about 2 minutes. Press the Cancel button, stir in clams, cream, and salt. Discard bay leaf and serve immediately with chives for garnish.

PER SERVING

CALORIES: 416 | FAT: 29g | PROTEIN: 15g | SODIUM: 312mg
FIBER: 1g | CARBOHYDRATES: 19g | SUGAR: 3g

Potato Corn Chowder

This chowder is more affordable than seafood-based chowders, but it's just as tasty. If you want to add additional savory flavor, sauté 1 cup of chopped ham or 4 strips of bacon (chopped) with the vegetables at the start of cooking.

- **Hands-On Time: 15 minutes**
- **Cook Time: 15 minutes**

Serves 8

4 tablespoons unsalted butter

2 stalks celery, chopped

1 medium carrot, peeled and chopped

1 medium yellow onion, peeled and diced

2 cloves garlic, peeled and minced

½ teaspoon ground black pepper

¼ teaspoon dried thyme

⅓ cup all-purpose flour

4 cups Chicken Stock (see recipe in Chapter 2)

1 bay leaf

1 pound russet potatoes, peeled and diced

2 cups fresh or frozen corn kernels

2 cups heavy cream

¼ cup chopped fresh flat-leaf parsley

1 Press the Sauté button on the Instant Pot® and melt butter. Add celery, carrot, and onion and cook until tender, about 5 minutes. Add garlic, pepper, and thyme and cook until fragrant, about 30 seconds.

2 Sprinkle flour over vegetables and mix well, then cook 1 minute until no dry flour remains. Slowly add stock, whisking constantly until smooth, then add bay leaf and potatoes. Press the Cancel button.

3 Close lid and set steam release to Sealing, then press the Manual button and adjust cook time to 5 minutes.

4 When the timer beeps, let pressure release naturally, about 15 minutes. Open lid and stir in corn and cream. Let chowder stand on the Keep Warm setting for 10 minutes, then discard bay leaf and serve immediately with parsley for garnish.

PER SERVING

CALORIES: 370 | FAT: 27g | PROTEIN: 6g | SODIUM: 50mg
FIBER: 2g | CARBOHYDRATES: 25g | SUGAR: 5g

Corn and Poblano Chowder

Poblano peppers are popular in Mexican and Southwest cuisine, and they are relatively mild when it comes to their level of spice.

- **Hands-On Time: 15 minutes**
- **Cook Time: 15 minutes**

Serves 8

4 tablespoons unsalted butter

2 medium poblano peppers, seeded and chopped

2 stalks celery, chopped

1 medium yellow onion, peeled and diced

2 cloves garlic, minced

½ teaspoon black pepper

½ teaspoon ground cumin

¼ teaspoon ground coriander

⅓ cup all-purpose flour

4 cups Chicken Stock (see recipe in Chapter 2)

1 bay leaf

1 pound russet potatoes, peeled and diced

2 cups corn kernels

2 cups heavy cream

¼ cup chopped fresh cilantro

COOKING WITH A THICKENER

It's best to save thickening a soup or stew in the Instant Pot® until after cooking has completed because a thickener may sink to the bottom and prevent the pot from coming up to pressure. If you do need to add flour before pressure cooking, be sure to scrape the bottom of the pot and keep the liquid moving.

1 Press the Sauté button on the Instant Pot® and melt butter. Add poblano peppers, celery, and onion and cook until tender, about 8 minutes. Add garlic, black pepper, cumin, and coriander and cook until fragrant, about 30 seconds.

2 Sprinkle flour over vegetables and mix well, then cook 1 minute until no dry flour remains. Slowly add stock, whisking constantly until smooth, then add bay leaf and potatoes. Press the Cancel button.

3 Close lid and set steam release to Sealing, then press the Manual button and adjust cook time to 5 minutes.

4 When the timer beeps, let pressure release naturally, about 15 minutes. Open lid and stir in corn and cream. Let chowder stand on the Keep Warm setting for 10 minutes, then discard bay leaf and serve immediately with cilantro for garnish.

PER SERVING

CALORIES: 379 | FAT: 28g | PROTEIN: 6g | SODIUM: 45mg
FIBER: 3g | CARBOHYDRATES: 26g | SUGAR: 5g

Shrimp Chowder with Corn

All you need to make this chowder a complete meal is a few hunks of crusty Italian or French bread for dipping. If you have cooked shrimp on hand, you can use them instead of raw shrimp; just let the chowder sit on the Keep Warm setting for 5–10 minutes to heat the shrimp through rather than simmering the soup.

- **Hands-On Time: 15 minutes**
- **Cook Time: 13 minutes**

Serves 8

4 tablespoons unsalted butter

2 stalks celery, chopped

1 medium carrot, peeled and chopped

1 medium yellow onion, peeled and diced

3 cloves garlic, peeled and minced

½ teaspoon ground black pepper

½ teaspoon seafood seasoning

⅓ cup all-purpose flour

4 cups Chicken Stock (see recipe in Chapter 2)

1 bay leaf

½ pound russet potatoes, peeled and diced

1 pound raw shrimp, peeled, deveined, and roughly chopped

2 cups fresh or frozen corn kernels

2 cups heavy cream

¼ cup chopped fresh flat-leaf parsley

1 Press the Sauté button on the Instant Pot® and melt butter. Add celery, carrot, and onion and cook until tender, about 8 minutes. Add garlic, pepper, and seafood seasoning and cook until fragrant, about 30 seconds.

2 Sprinkle flour over vegetables and mix well, then cook 1 minute until no dry flour remains. Slowly add stock, whisking constantly until smooth, then add bay leaf and potatoes. Press the Cancel button.

3 Close lid and set steam release to Sealing, then press the Manual button and adjust cook time to 5 minutes.

4 When the timer beeps, let pressure release naturally, about 15 minutes. Open lid and stir in shrimp and corn. Press the Cancel button, then press the Sauté button and allow soup to simmer, stirring often, until shrimp are cooked through, about 8 minutes.

5 Press the Cancel button, discard bay leaf, and stir in cream. Serve immediately with parsley for garnish.

PER SERVING

CALORIES: 390 | FAT: 28g | PROTEIN: 13g | SODIUM: 369mg
FIBER: 2g | CARBOHYDRATES: 21g | SUGAR: 5g

Sausage and Chicken Chowder

Cooking the sausage until it's crisp adds drippings to the pot, which adds flavor to the vegetables. It also gives the sausage firmer texture when compared to the tender chicken.

- **Hands-On Time: 15 minutes**
- **Cook Time: 10 minutes**

Serves 8

2 tablespoons unsalted butter

12 ounces beef sausage, diced

1 stalk celery, chopped

1 medium yellow onion, peeled and diced

2 cloves garlic, minced

¼ teaspoon dried sage

¼ teaspoon dried thyme

½ teaspoon ground black pepper

1 pound boneless, skinless chicken breast, diced

4 cups Chicken Stock (see recipe in Chapter 2)

1 (28-ounce) can crushed tomatoes

1 bay leaf

1 Press the Sauté button on the Instant Pot® and melt butter. Add sausage and cook until just starting to brown around the edges, about 6 minutes. Add celery and onion and cook until tender, about 5 minutes. Add garlic, sage, thyme, and pepper and cook until fragrant, about 30 seconds.

2 Add chicken, stock, tomatoes, and bay leaf. Stir well, then press the Cancel button.

3 Close lid and set steam release to Sealing, then press the Manual button and adjust cook time to 10 minutes. When the timer beeps, quick-release the pressure. Open lid and discard bay leaf. Serve immediately.

PER SERVING

CALORIES: 314 | FAT: 18g | PROTEIN: 22g | SODIUM: 568mg
FIBER: 2g | CARBOHYDRATES: 9g | SUGAR: 5g

RED VS. WHITE CHOWDER

In general there are two types of chowders: Manhattan chowders are thinner and tomato based. New England–style chowder is made with a thickened flour base, enriched with milk or cream. The debate over the "proper" type can be heated—there was even a Maine law proposed in the 1930s to make tomato-based chowders illegal!

Mushroom and Chicken Chowder

Chicken and mushrooms are a classic combination, and this chowder lets the power combo shine. Cremini mushrooms are called for here, but you can use a mix of any fresh mushrooms you like, so feel free to use mushrooms you like best. If you like, add ½ pound of scrubbed baby new potatoes or baby Yukon Gold potatoes cut in half.

- **Hands-On Time: 15 minutes**
- **Cook Time: 18 minutes**

Serves 8

3 tablespoons unsalted butter

2 stalks celery, chopped

1 medium carrot, peeled and chopped

1 medium yellow onion, peeled and diced

1 medium green bell pepper, seeded and chopped

4 cups sliced cremini mushrooms

2 cloves garlic, peeled and minced

½ teaspoon salt

½ teaspoon ground black pepper

¼ teaspoon dried thyme

⅓ cup all-purpose flour

4 cups Chicken Stock (see recipe in Chapter 2)

1 bay leaf

1 tablespoon sherry

1 pound boneless, skinless chicken thighs, cut into ½" pieces

2 cups heavy cream

⅓ cup chopped fresh flat-leaf parsley

1. Press the Sauté button on the Instant Pot® and melt butter. Add celery, carrot, onion, bell pepper, and mushrooms. Cook until tender, about 10 minutes. Add garlic, salt, black pepper, and thyme and cook until fragrant, about 30 seconds.

2. Sprinkle flour over vegetables and mix well, then cook 1 minute until no dry flour remains. Slowly add stock, whisking constantly until smooth, then add bay leaf, sherry, and chicken. Press the Cancel button.

3. Close lid and set steam release to Sealing, then press the Manual button and adjust cook time to 8 minutes.

4. When the timer beeps, let pressure release naturally, about 15 minutes. Open lid and stir in cream. Let chowder sit on the Keep Warm setting for 10 minutes. Discard bay leaf and serve immediately with parsley for garnish.

PER SERVING

CALORIES: 364 | FAT: 28g | PROTEIN: 15g | SODIUM: 255mg FIBER: 1g | CARBOHYDRATES: 11g | SUGAR: 4g

Ham Chowder

This chowder is a fun and unique way to use up leftover ham. Spiral-sliced hams, for example, are popular during winter and spring holidays, and while ham sandwiches are delicious, they can get a little old, and one can eat only so many ham and cheese omelets. Any kind of ham will work here, so don't worry if your ham is smoked, glazed, or simply baked. If you don't have leftover ham, look for diced ham in your grocery store's deli section.

- **Hands-On Time: 20 minutes**
- **Cook Time: 8 minutes**

Serves 8

8 slices thick-cut bacon, chopped

1 medium carrot, peeled and chopped

1 medium yellow onion, peeled and diced

2 cloves garlic, peeled and minced

½ teaspoon salt

½ teaspoon ground black pepper

¼ teaspoon dried thyme

⅓ cup all-purpose flour

4 cups Chicken Stock (see recipe in Chapter 2)

1 pound russet potatoes, peeled and diced

2 cups diced ham

1 bay leaf

2 cups heavy cream

2 cups shredded Cheddar cheese

⅓ cup chopped fresh flat-leaf parsley

1 Press the Sauté button on the Instant Pot® and add bacon. Cook until bacon has rendered fat and is starting to crisp, about 8 minutes. Add carrot and onion and cook until tender, about 5 minutes. Add garlic, salt, pepper, and thyme and cook until fragrant, about 30 seconds.

2 Sprinkle flour over vegetables and mix well, then cook 1 minute until no dry flour remains. Slowly add stock, whisking constantly until smooth, then add potatoes, ham, and bay leaf. Press the Cancel button.

3 Close lid and set steam release to Sealing, then press the Manual button and adjust cook time to 8 minutes.

4 When the timer beeps, let pressure release naturally, about 15 minutes. Open lid and stir in cream, then whisk in cheese until melted. Discard bay leaf and serve immediately with parsley for garnish.

PER SERVING

CALORIES: 599 | FAT: 45g | PROTEIN: 23g | SODIUM: 952mg
FIBER: 1g | CARBOHYDRATES: 19g | SUGAR: 4g

Shrimp Gumbo

Shrimp's popularity makes it easy to find in almost every grocery store. If you are able to source fresh shrimp from your fishmonger then use those, but frozen shrimp will work just as well. If using fresh shrimp, buy them the day you plan to cook them. Before cooking store fresh shrimp in a large bowl filled with crushed ice to preserve their freshness.

- Hands-On Time: 25 minutes
- Cook Time: 16 minutes

Serves 8

¼ cup vegetable oil

¼ cup all-purpose flour

4 stalks celery, chopped

1 large yellow onion, peeled and diced

1 large green bell pepper, seeded and diced

2 cloves garlic, peeled and minced

1 (14.5-ounce) can diced tomatoes

¼ teaspoon dried thyme

¼ teaspoon cayenne pepper

2 bay leaves

1 tablespoon filé powder

2 teaspoons Worcestershire sauce

4 cups Seafood Stock (see recipe in Chapter 2)

1 pound smoked sausage, sliced

1 pound medium shrimp, peeled and deveined

¼ teaspoon salt

¼ teaspoon ground black pepper

2 cups cooked long-grain rice

1 Press the Sauté button on the Instant Pot® and heat oil. Add flour and cook, stirring constantly, until flour is medium brown in color, about 15 minutes.

2 Add celery, onion, green pepper, garlic, and tomatoes and cook, stirring constantly, until the vegetables are tender, about 8 minutes. Add thyme, cayenne, bay leaves, filé, Worcestershire sauce, and stock and stir well, making sure nothing is stuck to the bottom of the pot, then add sausage. Press the Cancel button.

3 Close lid and set steam release to Sealing, then press the Manual button and adjust cook time to 8 minutes. When the timer beeps, quick-release the pressure. Open lid and stir in shrimp, salt, and black pepper. Press the Cancel button, then press the Sauté button and cook for 8 minutes, or until shrimp are cooked through. Discard bay leaves. Serve hot over rice.

PER SERVING

CALORIES: 389 | FAT: 22g | PROTEIN: 19g | SODIUM: 1,194mg FIBER: 2g | CARBOHYDRATES: 22g | SUGAR: 3g

Crawfish Gumbo

Crawfish, also known as crayfish, crawdads, or mudbugs, are freshwater crustaceans that can be found in various varieties all around the world. In North America, crawfish are commonly associated with Cajun cuisine where they are included in gumbos and étouffées, and as the star of a crawfish boil. The tail of the crawfish has the bulk of the meat, and you can find tail meat parcooked and frozen in most supermarkets, particularly in the southern part of the United States.

- **Hands-On Time: 30 minutes**
- **Cook Time: 18 minutes**

Serves 8

¼ cup vegetable oil

¼ cup all-purpose flour

4 stalks celery, chopped

1 large yellow onion, peeled and diced

1 green bell pepper, seeded and diced

3 cloves garlic, minced

1 (15-ounce) can diced tomatoes

½ teaspoon thyme

½ teaspoon Creole seasoning

3 bay leaves

2 tablespoons filé powder

2 tablespoons Worcestershire sauce

1 teaspoon hot sauce

4 cups Chicken Broth (see recipe in Chapter 2)

1 pound smoked sausage, sliced

2 cups parboiled crawfish tails

¼ teaspoon salt

¼ teaspoon ground black pepper

2 cups cooked long-grain rice

1 Press the Sauté button on the Instant Pot® and heat oil. Add flour and cook, stirring constantly, until flour is medium brown in color, about 15 minutes.

2 Add celery, onion, green pepper, garlic, and tomatoes and cook, stirring constantly, until the vegetables are tender, about 8 minutes. Add thyme, Creole seasoning, bay leaves, filé, Worcestershire sauce, hot sauce, and broth and stir well, making sure nothing is stuck to the bottom of the pot, then add sausage. Press the Cancel button.

3 Close lid and set steam release to Sealing, then press the Manual button and adjust cook time to 8 minutes. When the timer beeps, quick-release the pressure. Open lid and stir in crawfish, salt, and black pepper, then let stand on the Keep Warm setting for 10 minutes. Discard bay leaves. Serve hot over rice.

PER SERVING

CALORIES: 402 | FAT: 22g | PROTEIN: 21g | SODIUM: 1,887mg
FIBER: 2g | CARBOHYDRATES: 23g | SUGAR: 4g

Okra Gumbo

Fresh okra is available at its best from July to September in the United States. Look for pods that are bright green, unblemished, and firm but not too hard. If you can't find fresh okra, you can use frozen chopped okra. To help frozen okra retain its texture, add it along with the liquid, not at the start of cooking as directed in the recipe.

- **Hands-On Time: 25 minutes**
- **Cook Time: 8 minutes**

Serves 8

¼ cup vegetable oil

¼ cup all-purpose flour

4 stalks celery, chopped

1 large yellow onion, peeled and diced

1 large green bell pepper, seeded and diced

2 cups sliced fresh okra

3 cloves garlic, peeled and minced

½ teaspoon dried thyme

¼ teaspoon Creole seasoning

2 bay leaves

2 teaspoons Worcestershire sauce

4 cups Vegetable Broth (see recipe in Chapter 2)

¼ teaspoon salt

¼ teaspoon ground black pepper

2 cups cooked long-grain rice

1 Press the Sauté button on the Instant Pot® and heat oil. Add flour and cook, stirring constantly, until flour is medium brown in color, about 15 minutes.

2 Add celery, onion, green pepper, okra, and garlic and cook, stirring constantly, until the vegetables are tender, about 5 minutes. Add thyme, Creole seasoning, bay leaves, Worcestershire sauce, and broth and stir well, making sure nothing is stuck to the bottom of the pot. Press the Cancel button.

3 Close lid and set steam release to Sealing, then press the Manual button and adjust cook time to 8 minutes. When the timer beeps, quick-release the pressure. Open lid and stir in salt and black pepper. Discard bay leaves. Serve hot over rice.

PER SERVING

CALORIES: 172 | FAT: 9g | PROTEIN: 3g | SODIUM: 153mg FIBER: 2g | CARBOHYDRATES: 21g | SUGAR: 2g

Vegetarian Gumbo

Red beans add heartiness and protein to this Vegetarian Gumbo, and mushrooms add an extra punch of umami flavor. If you like, you can add sliced vegan sausage or meatballs after cooking, press the Keep Warm button, and let sit for 10–15 minutes.

- **Hands-On Time: 30 minutes**
- **Cook Time: 5 minutes**

Serves 8

¼ cup vegetable oil

¼ cup all-purpose flour

4 stalks celery, chopped

1 large yellow onion, peeled and diced

1 large green bell pepper, seeded and diced

2 cups sliced fresh okra

8 ounces button mushrooms, quartered

3 cloves garlic, peeled and minced

½ teaspoon dried thyme

¼ teaspoon Creole seasoning

2 bay leaves

2 teaspoons Creole mustard

4 cups Vegetable Broth (see recipe in Chapter 2)

1 medium zucchini, diced

1 (16-ounce) can red beans, drained and rinsed

¼ teaspoon salt

¼ teaspoon ground black pepper

2 cups cooked long-grain rice

1 Press the Sauté button on the Instant Pot® and heat oil. Once hot add flour and cook, stirring constantly, until flour is medium brown in color, about 15 minutes.

2 Add celery, onion, green pepper, okra, mushrooms, and garlic. Cook, stirring constantly, until the vegetables are tender, about 8 minutes. Add thyme, Creole seasoning, bay leaves, Creole mustard, and broth and stir well, making sure nothing is stuck to the bottom of the pot. Add zucchini and beans and stir well. Press the Cancel button.

3 Close lid and set steam release to Sealing, then press the Manual button and adjust cook time to 5 minutes. When the timer beeps, quick-release the pressure. Open lid, discard bay leaves, and stir in salt and black pepper. Serve hot over rice.

PER SERVING

CALORIES: 224 | FAT: 9g | PROTEIN: 6g | SODIUM: 252mg
FIBER: 5g | CARBOHYDRATES: 30g | SUGAR: 3g

Andouille Gumbo

Andouille sausage is made from coarsely ground pork mixed with spices and aromatic vegetables. It's most commonly associated with Creole cuisine in the US, but has its roots in France. In the South it is common to find andouille sausage, but if you can't find it in your market you can substitute your favorite pork sausage, such as kielbasa.

- **Hands-On Time: 25 minutes**
- **Cook Time: 5 minutes**

Serves 8

¼ cup vegetable oil

¼ cup all-purpose flour

4 stalks celery, chopped

1 large yellow onion, peeled and diced

1 large green bell pepper, seeded and diced

1 cup sliced fresh okra

3 cloves garlic, peeled and minced

½ teaspoon dried thyme

½ teaspoon Creole seasoning

2 pounds andouille sausage, sliced

2 bay leaves

2 teaspoons Worcestershire sauce

4 cups Chicken Broth (see recipe in Chapter 2)

¼ teaspoon salt

¼ teaspoon ground black pepper

2 cups cooked long-grain rice

1 Press the Sauté button on the Instant Pot® and heat oil. Add flour and cook, stirring constantly, until flour is medium brown in color, about 15 minutes.

2 Add celery, onion, green pepper, okra, and garlic and cook, stirring constantly, until the vegetables are tender, about 5 minutes. Add thyme, Creole seasoning, and sausage. Cook for 5 minutes, or until the sausage is hot, then add bay leaves, Worcestershire sauce, and broth and stir well, making sure nothing is stuck to the bottom of the pot. Press the Cancel button.

3 Close lid and set steam release to Sealing, then press the Manual button and adjust cook time to 5 minutes. When the timer beeps, quick-release the pressure. Open lid and stir in salt and black pepper. Discard bay leaves. Serve hot over rice.

PER SERVING

CALORIES: 395 | FAT: 26g | PROTEIN: 22g | SODIUM: 1,511mg
FIBER: 4g | CARBOHYDRATES: 22g | SUGAR: 2g

Chicken and Sausage Gumbo

A good gumbo starts with a good roux. While it takes a little time to prepare, the time it takes pays off in complex, rich flavor. The darker a roux becomes the less thickening power it has, and in this recipe the roux has a golden brown color, which strikes the right balance between flavor and thickness.

- **Hands-On Time: 30 minutes**
- **Cook Time: 18 minutes**

Serves 8

¼ cup vegetable oil

¼ cup all-purpose flour

4 stalks celery, chopped

1 large yellow onion, peeled and diced

1 large green bell pepper, seeded and diced

1 cup sliced fresh okra

4 cloves garlic, peeled and minced

1 (14.5-ounce) can diced tomatoes

½ teaspoon dried thyme

½ teaspoon Creole seasoning

3 bay leaves

2 tablespoons filé powder

2 teaspoons Worcestershire sauce

1 teaspoon hot sauce

4 cups Chicken Broth (see recipe in Chapter 2)

1 pound smoked sausage, sliced

2 cups shredded cooked chicken

¼ teaspoon salt

¼ teaspoon ground black pepper

2 cups cooked long-grain rice

1. Press the Sauté button on the Instant Pot® and heat oil. Add flour and cook, stirring constantly, until flour is medium brown in color, about 15 minutes.

2. Add celery, onion, green pepper, okra, garlic, and tomatoes and cook, stirring constantly, until the vegetables are tender, about 8 minutes. Add thyme, Creole seasoning, bay leaves, filé, Worcestershire sauce, hot sauce, and broth and stir well, making sure nothing is stuck to the bottom of the pot, then add sausage. Press the Cancel button.

3. Close lid and set steam release to Sealing, then press the Manual button and adjust cook time to 8 minutes. When the timer beeps, quick-release the pressure. Open lid, discard bay leaves, and stir in chicken, salt, and black pepper. Let stand on the Keep Warm setting for 10 minutes. Serve hot over rice.

PER SERVING

CALORIES: 418 | FAT: 23.5g | PROTEIN: 22g | SODIUM: 840mg
FIBER: 3g | CARBOHYDRATES: 23g | SUGAR: 3g

8

Stews

Stews can be found, in one form or another, all around the world. Different cultures have their distinct takes on the humble stew, transforming it into something universally appealing. At its most basic, stew is a dish of meat and vegetables slowly cooked in a thick and flavorful gravy until tender.

Most stew recipes take a few hours to properly prepare. Some are simmered on the stove; others are baked in the oven. The common denominator in all these recipes is time. The Instant Pot® has changed all that! Now, stew can be prepared and ready to serve in about an hour, sometimes less, with the same tender meat and vegetables and the same savory gravy. Even better, everything is made in the same pot, so there aren't loads of dishes to wash when you are done.

No matter what stew you make, your Instant Pot® will make it faster and easier while still retaining everything that makes stew special.

Classic Beef Stew

Traditional beef stew recipes call for simmering, or baking, the stew in a Dutch oven for hours. This long cooking time makes the beef chunks tender and helps the flavors of the stew to combine. It also makes it difficult to have beef stew without a lot of prior planning. The Instant Pot® slashes that time to under an hour, so you can have a hearty beef stew supper any time you like.

- **Hands-On Time: 30 minutes**
- **Cook Time: 35 minutes**

Serves 6

1 pound beef stew meat, cut into 1" cubes

¼ cup all-purpose flour

1 teaspoon salt

1 teaspoon ground black pepper

3 tablespoons olive oil

2 tablespoons tomato paste

1 teaspoon dried thyme leaves

3 cups Beef Broth (see recipe in Chapter 2)

1 teaspoon Worcestershire sauce

3 cloves garlic, peeled and minced

1 (8-ounce) container sliced button mushrooms

3 medium carrots, peeled and cut into ½" pieces

1 medium yellow onion, peeled and roughly chopped

1 large russet potato, peeled and cut into ½" cubes

1 In a zip-top bag or airtight storage container, add beef, flour, salt, and pepper. Shake to coat beef cubes evenly.

2 Press the Sauté button on the Instant Pot® and heat oil. Add half the beef to pot in an even layer, making sure there is space between beef cubes to prevent steam from forming. Brown 3 minutes on each side. Remove from pot and reserve on a plate. Repeat with remaining beef.

3 Add tomato paste and thyme to pot and cook 30 seconds, then add broth and scrape pot to release any browned bits. Press the Cancel button.

4 Add beef cubes and remaining ingredients to pot. Close lid, set steam release to Sealing, press the Manual button, and adjust cook time to 35 minutes.

5 When the timer beeps, let pressure release naturally, about 20 minutes. Press the Cancel button, open lid, and stir well. If you prefer a thicker stew, press the Sauté button and let stew reduce to desired thickness. Serve hot.

PER SERVING

CALORIES: 270 | FAT: 11g | PROTEIN: 21g | SODIUM: 634mg
FIBER: 3g | CARBOHYDRATES: 23g | SUGAR: 4g

Guinness Stew

This Irish pub classic is the definition of comfort food. It's perfect with slices of Irish soda bread, butter, and (of course) a well-built pint of Guinness.

- **Hands-On Time: 30 minutes**
- **Cook Time: 35 minutes**

Serves 8

2 pounds boneless beef chuck steak, cubed

2 tablespoons all-purpose flour

½ teaspoon salt

¼ teaspoon black pepper

2 tablespoons vegetable oil

1 medium onion, peeled and chopped

1 clove garlic, chopped

½ teaspoon dried thyme

1 cup Guinness stout

1 cup Beef Broth (see recipe in Chapter 2)

1 bay leaf

2 large carrots, peeled and chopped

2 medium russet potatoes, chopped

¼ cup chopped fresh flat-leaf parsley

STEW IN IRELAND

Traditional Irish stew was made with lamb or mutton. Guinness adds deep caramel flavor and helps tenderize tougher cuts of meat. Today Guinness stew is commonly made with beef, and in pubs you will usually see beef and Guinness stews on the menu.

1 In a medium bowl add the beef, flour, salt, and pepper. Toss meat with seasoned flour until thoroughly coated. Set aside.

2 Press the Sauté button on the Instant Pot® and heat oil. Once the oil is hot add half the beef to pot in an even layer, making sure there is space between beef cubes to prevent steam from forming. Brown 3 minutes on each side. Remove from pot and reserve on a plate. Repeat with remaining beef.

3 Add the onion, garlic, and thyme to pot and cook until the onion is tender, about 5 minutes, then add half the Guinness and scrape off all the browned bits from the bottom of the pot. Add the remaining Guinness, broth, bay leaf, carrots, potatoes, and the browned beef along with any juices that have accumulated on plate. Press the Cancel button.

4 Close lid, set steam release to Sealing, press the Manual button, and adjust cook time to 35 minutes. When the timer beeps, let pressure release naturally, about 20 minutes. Press the Cancel button, open lid, and stir well. If you prefer a thicker stew, press the Sauté button and let stew reduce to desired thickness. Discard the bay leaf, and serve hot with fresh parsley as a garnish.

PER SERVING

CALORIES: 249 | **FAT:** 9g | **PROTEIN:** 27g | **SODIUM:** 280mg
FIBER: 2g | **CARBOHYDRATES:** 15g | **SUGAR:** 2g

Chicken Stew

Chicken thighs have a richer flavor and stand up to the hearty flavors in this stew better than breast meat. That said, if you prefer chicken breast you can swap it here, just be sure to watch it while it is browning. A light golden brown color is all you need for breast meat, but thighs can be more robustly browned.

- **Hands-On Time: 25 minutes**
- **Cook Time: 20 minutes**

Serves 6

1 pound boneless, skinless chicken thighs, cut into 1" pieces

¼ cup all-purpose flour

1 teaspoon salt

1 teaspoon ground black pepper

3 tablespoons olive oil

2 cloves garlic, peeled and minced

1 teaspoon dried thyme leaves

½ teaspoon poultry seasoning

3 cups Chicken Broth (see recipe in Chapter 2)

3 medium carrots, peeled and diced

2 stalks celery, chopped

1 medium yellow onion, peeled and chopped

2 medium red potatoes, cut into ½" cubes

1 In a zip-top bag or airtight storage container, add chicken, flour, salt, and pepper. Shake to coat chicken evenly.

2 Press the Sauté button on the Instant Pot® and heat oil. Add half the chicken to pot in an even layer, making sure there is space between pieces to prevent steam from forming. Brown 3 minutes on each side. Remove from pot and reserve on a plate. Repeat with remaining chicken.

3 Add garlic, thyme, and poultry seasoning to pot and cook 30 seconds, then add broth and scrape pot to release any browned bits. Press the Cancel button.

4 Add chicken pieces and remaining ingredients to Instant Pot®. Close lid, set steam release to Sealing, press the Manual button, and adjust cook time to 20 minutes.

5 When the timer beeps, let pressure release naturally, about 20 minutes. Press the Cancel button, open lid, and stir well. If you prefer a thicker stew, press the Sauté setting and let stew reduce to desired thickness. Serve hot.

PER SERVING

CALORIES: 254 | FAT: 10g | PROTEIN: 18g | SODIUM: 508mg
FIBER: 3g | CARBOHYDRATES: 21g | SUGAR: 3g

Cioppino

Cioppino originated in San Francisco in the late 1880s. Italian immigrants would invite their friends and neighbors to come for seafood stew and to bring what bits of seafood they had on hand. Usually it is made with a mix of mussels, clams, scallops, shrimp, and crab in a white wine and tomato-based broth. You can use any seafood here that you like, so use what you and your family like best.

- **Hands-On Time: 15 minutes**
- **Cook Time: 15 minutes**

Serves 8

2 tablespoons unsalted butter

2 stalks celery, chopped

1 medium yellow onion, peeled and diced

1 medium red bell pepper, seeded and diced

3 cloves garlic, minced

1 teaspoon dried oregano

½ teaspoon Italian seasoning

½ teaspoon black pepper

½ teaspoon salt

2 tablespoons tomato paste

1 cup white wine

1 (15-ounce) can crushed tomatoes

4 cups Seafood Stock (see recipe in Chapter 2)

1 bay leaf

1 pound fresh mussels, scrubbed clean and beards removed

1 pound fresh clams, scrubbed clean

½ pound large shrimp, peeled and deveined

½ pound fresh scallops

½ pound calamari rings

1 tablespoon lemon juice

1. Press the Sauté button on the Instant Pot® and melt butter. Add celery, onion, and bell pepper and cook until tender, about 8 minutes. Add garlic, oregano, Italian seasoning, black pepper, and salt and cook for 30 seconds. Add tomato paste and cook for 1 minute, then slowly pour in wine and scrape bottom of pot well. Press the Cancel button.

2. Add tomatoes, stock, and bay leaf. Stir well. Close lid and set steam release to Sealing, then press the Manual button and adjust cook time to 5 minutes.

3. When the timer beeps, quick-release pressure. Open lid and stir in mussels, clams, shrimp, scallops, and calamari. Press the Cancel button, then press the Sauté button and allow soup to simmer until seafood is cooked through, about 10 minutes. Discard bay leaf and stir in lemon juice. Serve hot.

PER SERVING

CALORIES: 188 | FAT: 4g | PROTEIN: 22g | SODIUM: 1,147mg
FIBER: 2g | CARBOHYDRATES: 12g | SUGAR: 4g

Fish and Potato Stew

This Irish-inspired stew is both hearty and delicate. If you are not a fan of beer, you can swap it out for Vegetable Broth (see recipe in Chapter 2) or water. Serve this stew right away with hunks of crusty bread slathered with plenty of salted butter, and a cold glass of beer.

- **Hands-On Time: 15 minutes**
- **Cook Time: 20 minutes**

Serves 8

2 tablespoons unsalted butter

2 stalks celery, chopped

1 medium yellow onion, peeled and diced

1 medium carrot, peeled and diced

2 cloves garlic, peeled and minced

1 teaspoon Italian seasoning

¼ teaspoon dried thyme

¼ teaspoon ground black pepper

¼ teaspoon salt

1 cup lager-style beer

1 (28-ounce) can diced tomatoes

3 cups Seafood Stock (see recipe in Chapter 2)

1 bay leaf

2 large russet potatoes, peeled and diced

2 pounds whitefish (haddock, cod, or catfish), cut into 1" pieces

2 tablespoons lemon juice

1. Press the Sauté button on the Instant Pot® and melt butter. Add celery, onion and carrot and cook until tender, about 8 minutes. Add garlic, Italian seasoning, thyme, pepper, and salt and cook for 30 seconds. Add beer and scrape bottom of pot well. Press the Cancel button.

2. Add tomatoes, stock, bay leaf, and potatoes. Stir well. Close lid and set steam release to Sealing, then press the Manual button and adjust cook time to 10 minutes.

3. When the timer beeps, quick-release the pressure. Open lid and stir in fish. Press the Cancel button, then press the Sauté button and allow soup to simmer until seafood is cooked through, about 10 minutes. Discard bay leaf and stir in lemon juice. Serve hot.

PER SERVING

CALORIES: 224 | FAT: 3g | PROTEIN: 22g | SODIUM: 573mg
FIBER: 3g | CARBOHYDRATES: 24g | SUGAR: 4g

Chicken and Dumplings

The homemade flat dumplings in this stew are like a thick noodle in texture. If you prefer the fluffy biscuit-style dumplings, you can use store-bought biscuit mix. Prepare the mix for dumplings, drop them by heaping tablespoons into the pot, and cook as directed in the recipe. Be sure to gently stir dumplings to avoid breaking them up.

- Hands-On Time: 25 minutes
- Cook Time: 30 minutes

Serves 8

1⅓ cups all-purpose flour

2 tablespoons unsalted butter

2 teaspoons baking powder

½ teaspoon salt

2 large eggs, beaten

¼ cup whole milk

2 pounds boneless, skinless chicken breasts, cut into 1" pieces

1 medium onion, peeled and chopped

2 stalks celery, chopped

1 medium carrot, peeled and chopped

½ teaspoon salt

½ teaspoon ground black pepper

½ teaspoon poultry seasoning

1 bay leaf

4 cups Chicken Stock (see recipe in Chapter 2)

½ cup half-and-half

½ cup frozen peas

1 In a large bowl combine flour, butter, baking powder, and salt. With your fingers rub the butter into the flour mixture until it resembles coarse sand. Add eggs and milk and mix until mixture forms into a dough ball. Roll out to ⅛" thick and cut into 1" strips. Cover with a tea towel until ready to use.

2 Place chicken, onion, celery, carrot, salt, pepper, poultry seasoning, bay leaf, and stock in the Instant Pot®. Close lid, set steam release to Sealing, press the Manual button, and adjust cook time to 15 minutes. When the timer beeps, let pressure release naturally, about 20 minutes.

3 Press the Cancel button, open lid, discard bay leaf, and add prepared dumplings. Close lid, set steam release to Sealing, press the Manual button, and set time to 5 minutes. When the timer beeps, quick-release the pressure. Open lid and stir in half-and-half and peas. Let stand, uncovered, on the Keep Warm setting for 10 minutes. Serve hot.

PER SERVING

CALORIES: 287 | FAT: 8g | PROTEIN: 31g | SODIUM: 513mg
FIBER: 1g | CARBOHYDRATES: 17g | SUGAR: 3g

Green Lentil Stew

Chicken sausage is growing in popularity because it retains the delectable flavor of pork and beef sausages but with less fat and fewer calories. For this stew, look for a firm chicken sausage, preferably one without large chunks of vegetables or cheese. A chicken and apple sausage, for example, would be ideal. The gentle sweetness of the apple will pair well with the earthy green lentils.

- **Hands-On Time: 15 minutes**
- **Cook Time: 25 minutes**

Serves 6

2 tablespoons vegetable oil

1 pound chicken sausage, sliced

3 stalks celery, cut into ½" pieces

2 medium carrots, peeled and cut into ½" pieces

1 medium yellow onion, peeled and roughly chopped

2 cloves garlic, peeled and minced

½ teaspoon salt

2 cups green lentils

1 large russet potato, peeled and cut into ½" pieces

¼ cup chopped fresh flat-leaf parsley

4 cups Chicken Stock (see recipe in Chapter 2)

1 Press the Sauté button on the Instant Pot® and heat oil. Add sausage and cook until edges are browned, about 8 minutes. Transfer to a plate and set aside. To pot add celery, carrots, and onion. Cook until just tender, about 3 minutes. Add garlic and salt and cook until fragrant, about 30 seconds. Press the Cancel button.

2 Add sausage and remaining ingredients, close lid, set steam release to Sealing, press the Manual button and adjust time to 25 minutes. When the timer beeps, let pressure release naturally, about 15 minutes. Remove lid and stir. Serve warm.

PER SERVING

CALORIES: 477 | FAT: 12g | PROTEIN: 35g | SODIUM: 681mg
FIBER: 9g | CARBOHYDRATES: 56g | SUGAR: 4g

Chicken and Pinto Bean Stew

If you enjoy Mexican-style chicken and rice, then you are going to enjoy this stew. Canned pinto beans are used to help save time, but you can replace them with 1½ cups of dried pinto beans soaked overnight in water to cover, then drained. Add an extra cup of chicken broth or water, too, since the beans soak up some of the liquid while cooking, and add an additional 10 minutes to the cooking time.

- Hands-On Time: 25 minutes
- Cook Time: 20 minutes

Serves 6

1 pound boneless, skinless chicken thighs, cut into 1" pieces
¼ cup all-purpose flour
1 teaspoon salt
1 teaspoon ground black pepper
3 tablespoons olive oil
2 cloves garlic, peeled and minced
1 teaspoon ground cumin
½ teaspoon ground coriander
½ teaspoon chili powder
3 cups Chicken Broth (see recipe in Chapter 2)
2 medium carrots, peeled and diced
2 stalks celery, chopped
1 medium yellow onion, peeled and chopped
1 (15-ounce) can pinto beans, drained and rinsed
1 (10-ounce) can diced tomatoes with green chilies, drained

1 In a zip-top bag or airtight storage container, add chicken, flour, salt, and pepper. Shake to coat beef cubes evenly.

2 Press the Sauté button on the Instant Pot® and heat oil. Add half the chicken to pot in an even layer, making sure there is space between pieces to prevent steam from forming. Brown 3 minutes on each side. Remove from pot and reserve on a plate. Repeat with remaining chicken.

3 Add garlic, cumin, coriander, and chili powder to pot and cook 30 seconds, then add broth and scrape pot to release any browned bits. Press the Cancel button.

4 Add chicken pieces and remaining ingredients to the pot. Close lid, set steam release to Sealing, press the Manual button, and adjust cook time to 20 minutes.

5 When the timer beeps, let pressure release naturally, about 20 minutes. Press the Cancel button, open lid, and stir well. If you prefer a thicker stew, press the Sauté button and let stew reduce to desired thickness. Serve hot.

PER SERVING

CALORIES: 268 | FAT: 10g | PROTEIN: 21g | SODIUM: 743mg
FIBER: 2g | CARBOHYDRATES: 21g | SUGAR: 3g

Lamb and Vegetable Stew

Lamb has a mild, fresh flavor with grassy notes and mild sweetness. That sweetness is built upon in this recipe with baby carrots and peas. If you don't like lamb, you can use beef or pork in this recipe with great success.

- **Hands-On Time: 25 minutes**
- **Cook Time: 30 minutes**

Serves 6

2 pounds lean, boneless lamb shoulder, cut into 1" cubes

¼ teaspoon salt

¼ teaspoon ground black pepper

2 tablespoons olive oil

1 large onion, peeled and chopped

1 clove garlic, peeled and minced

¼ cup dry white wine

4 cups Chicken Stock (see recipe in Chapter 2)

1 bay leaf

1 teaspoon dried thyme

2 pounds small red potatoes, scrubbed and quartered

16 ounces sliced button mushrooms

8 ounces baby-cut carrots

8 ounces frozen peas

1 Season lamb with salt and pepper. Cover and refrigerate for 15 minutes.

2 Press the Sauté button on the Instant Pot® and heat oil. Add half the lamb in an even layer, making sure there is space between pieces to prevent steam from forming. Brown 3 minutes on each side. Remove from pot and reserve on a plate. Repeat with remaining lamb.

3 To pot add onion and garlic and cook for 1 minute, then add wine and scrape any bits from bottom of pot. Press the Cancel button. Add lamb, stock, bay leaf, thyme, potatoes, mushrooms, and carrots. Close lid, set steam release to Sealing, press the Manual button, and adjust cook time to 20 minutes.

4 When the timer beeps, let pressure release naturally, about 20 minutes. Open lid, discard bay leaf, stir in peas, and let stand on the Keep Warm setting for 10 minutes. Serve warm.

PER SERVING

CALORIES: 623 | FAT: 35g | PROTEIN: 34g | SODIUM: 294mg
FIBER: 6g | CARBOHYDRATES: 36g | SUGAR: 8g

Basque Lamb Stew

The Basque region is an area west of the Pyrenees on the border between France and Spain. The people of the region, called Basques, have a unique language, culture, and set of culinary traditions. Sweet peppers, paprika, and tomatoes are common in Basque cuisine, and all three are featured in this unique lamb stew.

- **Hands-On Time: 25 minutes**
- **Cook Time: 30 minutes**

Serves 6

2 pounds lamb shoulder, cut into 2" cubes

¼ teaspoon salt

¼ teaspoon ground black pepper

2 tablespoons olive oil

1 large onion, peeled and chopped

4 cloves garlic, peeled and minced

2 tablespoons sweet paprika

½ cup dry white wine

1 cup sliced roasted red peppers

2 Roma tomatoes, seeded and chopped

3 cups Chicken Stock (see recipe in Chapter 2)

1 cup red wine

1 bay leaf

1 sprig fresh rosemary

1 Season lamb with salt and pepper. Press the Sauté button on the Instant Pot® and heat oil. Add half the lamb in an even layer, making sure there is space between pieces to prevent steam from forming. Brown 3 minutes on each side. Remove from pot and reserve on a plate. Repeat with remaining lamb.

2 To pot add onion and garlic and cook for 1 minute, then add paprika and cook until paprika is slightly darker in color, about 2 minutes. Add white wine and scrape any bits from bottom of pot. Press the Cancel button. Add lamb along with remaining ingredients. Close lid, set steam release to Sealing, press the Manual button, and adjust cook time to 30 minutes.

3 Once cooking is complete allow pressure to release naturally, about 20 minutes. Open lid and stir well. Discard bay leaf and rosemary. Serve warm.

PER SERVING

CALORIES: 501 | **FAT:** 35g | **PROTEIN:** 27g | **SODIUM:** 517mg
FIBER: 2g | **CARBOHYDRATES:** 7g | **SUGAR:** 2g

Pozole

This Mexican pork stew is a celebratory dish, often served for special occasions and holidays. It contains hominy, which is dried field corn soaked in an alkali solution. After soaking, the corn is washed. It is then used for making masa, or used as is in soups and stews. Most markets sell canned hominy in the bean section or with the canned vegetables.

- **Hands-On Time: 30 minutes**
- **Cook Time: 35 minutes**

Serves 6

2½ pounds boneless pork shoulder, cut into 2" pieces

1 teaspoon salt, divided

1 teaspoon ground black pepper, divided

2 tablespoons vegetable oil

2 medium yellow onions, peeled and chopped

2 medium poblano peppers, seeded and diced

1 chipotle pepper in adobo, minced

1 cinnamon stick

4 cloves garlic, peeled and minced

1 tablespoon smoked paprika

2 teaspoons chili powder

1 teaspoon ground cumin

1 teaspoon dried oregano

½ teaspoon ground coriander

1 (12-ounce) can lager-style beer

4 cups Chicken Broth (see recipe in Chapter 2)

2 (15-ounce) cans hominy, drained and rinsed

1 tablespoon lime juice

½ cup chopped cilantro

1 Season pork pieces with ½ teaspoon salt and ½ teaspoon pepper. Press the Sauté button on the Instant Pot® and heat oil. Add half the pork to pot in an even layer, making sure there is space between pieces to prevent steam from forming. Brown 3 minutes on each side. Remove from pot and reserve on a plate. Repeat with remaining pork.

2 Add onions and poblano peppers to pot and cook until vegetables are just tender, about 5 minutes. Add chipotle pepper, cinnamon, garlic, paprika, chili powder, cumin, oregano, and coriander. Cook until spices and garlic are fragrant, about 1 minute. Return pork to pot and turn to coat with spices. Stir in beer and broth and press the Cancel button.

3 Close lid, set steam release to Sealing, press the Manual button, and adjust cook time to 35 minutes. Once cooking is complete allow pressure to release naturally, about 20 minutes. Press the Cancel button, open lid, and stir well. If you prefer a thicker stew, press the Sauté button and let stew reduce to desired thickness. Season with remaining salt and pepper, then stir in hominy, lime juice, and cilantro. Serve hot.

PER SERVING

CALORIES: 407 | FAT: 13g | PROTEIN: 43g | SODIUM: 1,016mg
FIBER: 6g | CARBOHYDRATES: 24g | SUGAR: 4g

Pork and Beer Stew

This sweet and savory pork stew uses tart apples. The sweet-tart flavor of the apples makes this stew perfect for the fall. You can make this a day or two ahead of time so the flavors can have more time to develop, then rewarm in your Instant Pot®. If you prefer, use chicken thighs or beef chuck instead of pork.

- Hands-On Time: 30 minutes
- Cook Time: 35 minutes

Serves 6

2 tablespoons vegetable oil

2 pounds boneless pork shoulder, cut into 2" pieces

1 medium yellow onion, peeled and chopped

1 medium carrot, peeled and chopped

1 stalk celery, chopped

1 Granny Smith apple, peeled, cored, and sliced

3 cloves garlic, peeled and minced

½ teaspoon dried thyme

2 tablespoons light brown sugar

3 cups Chicken Broth (see recipe in Chapter 2)

1 (12-ounce) bottle lager-style beer

½ teaspoon salt

½ teaspoon ground black pepper

6 cups cooked wide egg noodles

1 Press the Sauté button on the Instant Pot® and heat oil. Add half the pork to pot in an even layer, making sure there is space between pieces to prevent steam from forming. Brown 3 minutes on each side. Remove from pot and reserve on a plate. Repeat with remaining pork.

2 Add onion, carrot, celery, and apple. Cook, stirring frequently, until vegetables and apple are tender, about 8 minutes. Add garlic, thyme, and brown sugar and cook for 30 seconds.

3 Add browned pork, broth, and beer and stir well. Press the Cancel button. Close lid, set steam release to Sealing, press the Manual button, and adjust cook time to 35 minutes.

4 When the timer beeps, let pressure release naturally, about 20 minutes. Press the Cancel button, open lid, and stir well. If you prefer a thicker stew, press the Sauté button and let stew reduce to desired thickness. Season with salt and pepper. Serve hot over cooked egg noodles.

PER SERVING

CALORIES: 474 | FAT: 12g | PROTEIN: 39g | SODIUM: 811mg
FIBER: 3g | CARBOHYDRATES: 47g | SUGAR: 11g

Ropa Vieja

Traditionally, Ropa Vieja is made with flank steak, but it can be a little tough so a fattier meat, boneless chuck, is used here. The name *ropa vieja* translates to "old clothes," because the meat after cooking resembles old rags in a washtub. That may not sound delicious, but this stew has tremendous flavor. Serve it with fried plantains or ladled over mashed potatoes for an extra-hearty meal.

- **Hands-On Time: 45 minutes**
- **Cook Time: 40 minutes**

Serves 6

2½ pounds boneless chuck roast or brisket, cut into 4" pieces

1 teaspoon salt

1 teaspoon ground black pepper

1 tablespoon olive oil

2 medium yellow onions, peeled and chopped

2 medium red bell peppers, seeded and chopped

6 cloves garlic, peeled and minced

2 teaspoons dried oregano

2 teaspoons ground cumin

2 teaspoons smoked paprika

½ teaspoon cayenne pepper

½ cup white wine

1 (14.5-ounce) can diced tomatoes

1 bay leaf

½ cup halved Spanish olives

2 teaspoons distilled white vinegar

1. Season meat with salt and pepper on all sides. Set aside.

2. Press the Sauté button on the Instant Pot® and heat oil. Brown half the meat until well browned, about 7 minutes on each side. Transfer browned meat to a platter and set aside. Repeat with remaining meat.

3. Add onions and bell peppers to pot. Cook until vegetables are just tender, about 5 minutes. Add garlic, oregano, cumin, paprika, and cayenne pepper. Cook 1 minute until fragrant. Add wine and cook until liquid is reduced by half, about 2 minutes. Add tomatoes, bay leaf, and meat back to pot. Press the Cancel button.

4. Close lid and set steam release to Sealing, then press the Manual button and adjust cook time to 40 minutes. When the timer beeps, quick-release the pressure. Open lid and discard bay leaf. Stir in olives and vinegar, then shred meat with two forks. Serve hot.

PER SERVING

CALORIES: 331 | FAT: 10g | PROTEIN: 43g | SODIUM: 810mg
FIBER: 2g | CARBOHYDRATES: 9g | SUGAR: 4g

Cuban Black Bean Stew

To save time you can make this stew with canned black beans in place of the soaked dried beans. Use two 15-ounce cans that have been drained and rinsed and reduce the stock by 1 cup. Serve this stew over fresh-cooked white rice, along with lime wedges and fresh cilantro for garnish. To make it a little creamy, gently mash 1 cup of the beans after cooking, then stir them back into the pot.

- Hands-On Time: 20 minutes
- Cook Time: 30 minutes

Serves 6

2 tablespoons vegetable oil

8 slices thick-cut smoked bacon, chopped

1 medium green bell pepper, seeded and chopped

1 medium yellow onion, peeled and chopped

1 small jalapeño pepper, seeded and chopped

4 cloves garlic, peeled and minced

1 tablespoon light brown sugar

1 teaspoon ground cumin

½ teaspoon dried oregano

1 tablespoon white vinegar

1½ cups dried black beans, soaked overnight in water to cover and drained

6 cups Ham Stock (see recipe in Chapter 2)

1 teaspoon salt

1 teaspoon ground black pepper

1. Press the Sauté button on the Instant Pot® and heat oil. Add bacon and cook until fat begins to render and edges begin to brown, about 5 minutes. Add bell pepper, onion, and jalapeño. Cook, stirring frequently, until vegetables are tender, about 8 minutes.

2. Add garlic, brown sugar, cumin, and oregano to pot and cook 30 seconds, then add vinegar and scrape pot well. Press the Cancel button.

3. Add beans and stock to pot. Stir well. Close lid, set steam release to Sealing, press the Manual button, and adjust cook time to 30 minutes.

4. When the timer beeps, let pressure release naturally, about 20 minutes. Press the Cancel button, open lid, and stir well. If you prefer a thicker stew, press the Sauté button and let stew reduce to desired thickness. Season with salt and pepper. Serve hot.

PER SERVING

CALORIES: 448 | FAT: 25g | PROTEIN: 18g | SODIUM: 830mg
FIBER: 8g | CARBOHYDRATES: 36g | SUGAR: 5g

Pork, Chorizo, and Chickpea Stew

This Spanish-influenced stew is bursting with savory flavor from pork shoulder and chorizo. Spanish chorizo is a dry-cured sausage made in a casing. It differs from Mexican-style chorizo in that you can slice it like salami. If you can't find Spanish-style chorizo, you can use your favorite pork sausage and add an extra tablespoon of sweet paprika.

- **Hands-On Time: 35 minutes**
- **Cook Time: 35 minutes**

Serves 6

2 tablespoons vegetable oil

2 pounds boneless pork shoulder, cut into 2" pieces

1 pound Spanish chorizo, sliced

1 medium yellow onion, peeled and chopped

1 medium carrot, peeled and chopped

2 cloves garlic, peeled and minced

1 tablespoon smoked paprika

2 teaspoons hot paprika

2 (15-ounce) cans chickpeas, drained and rinsed

4 cups Chicken Broth (see recipe in Chapter 2)

1 (15-ounce) can crushed tomatoes

½ teaspoon salt

½ teaspoon ground black pepper

1 Press the Sauté button on the Instant Pot® and heat oil. Once hot add half the pork to pot in an even layer, making sure there is space between pieces to prevent steam from forming. Brown 3 minutes on each side. Remove from pot and reserve on a plate. Repeat with remaining pork.

2 Add chorizo to pot and cook until chorizo has rendered some fat and edges are browned, about 6 minutes. Add onion, carrot, garlic, smoked paprika, and hot paprika. Cook, stirring frequently, until vegetables are tender, about 8 minutes.

3 Add chickpeas, broth, and tomatoes and stir well, then add browned pork back to pot. Press the Cancel button. Close lid, set steam release to Sealing, press the Manual button, and adjust cook time to 35 minutes.

4 When the timer beeps, let pressure release naturally, about 20 minutes. Press the Cancel button, open lid, and stir well. If you prefer a thicker stew, press the Sauté button and let stew reduce to desired thickness. Season with salt and pepper. Serve hot.

PER SERVING

CALORIES: 743 | FAT: 40g | PROTEIN: 58g | SODIUM: 1,597mg
FIBER: 8g | CARBOHYDRATES: 31g | SUGAR: 8g

Chinese Soy Sauce Pork Belly Stew

Pork belly can be found at Asian markets, but is also available in many wholesale stores and gourmet markets. Serve it with stir-fried cabbage, snow peas, or mushrooms, or bok choy.

- **Hands-On Time: 25 minutes**
- **Cook Time: 30 minutes**

Serves 8

½ cup soy sauce

¼ cup Chinese cooking wine

½ cup packed light brown sugar

2 pounds pork belly, skinned and cut into 1" cubes

3 tablespoons vegetable oil

12 scallions, cut into 1" pieces

3 cloves garlic, minced

2 tablespoons soy sauce

1 teaspoon Chinese five-spice powder

2 cups Vegetable Broth (see recipe in Chapter 2)

4 cups cooked white rice

CHINESE FIVE-SPICE

You can make your own five-spice blend by mixing equal parts star anise, clove, cinnamon, Sichuan pepper, and fennel seeds in a spice grinder. For more flavor, toast the whole spices in a dry skillet before grinding. Store five-spice in the refrigerator for up to 6 months.

1. In a zip-top bag or airtight storage container, add soy sauce, wine, and brown sugar. Mix well, then add pork and turn to coat evenly. Refrigerate for at least 4 hours. Strain off marinade and reserve. Pat pork dry.

2. Press the Sauté button on the Instant Pot® and heat oil. Add half the pork to pot in an even layer, making sure there is space between pork cubes to prevent steam from forming. Brown 3 minutes on each side. Remove from pot and reserve on a plate. Repeat with remaining pork.

3. Press the Cancel button, then add remaining ingredients and browned pork to pot with reserved marinade. Close lid, set steam release to Sealing, press the Manual button, and adjust cook time to 30 minutes.

4. Once cooking is complete allow pressure to release naturally, about 20 minutes. Press the Cancel button, open lid, and stir well. If you prefer a thicker stew, press the Sauté button and let stew reduce to desired thickness. Serve hot over cooked rice.

PER SERVING

CALORIES: 718 | **FAT:** 56g | **PROTEIN:** 13g | **SODIUM:** 344mg
FIBER: 1g | **CARBOHYDRATES:** 31g | **SUGAR:** 2g

Filipino Beef Stew

Also known as *mechado*, this Filipino version of beef stew uses familiar ingredients along with Filipino flavors to create a unique dish. While this recipe calls for soy sauce, fish sauce is more authentic. You can find fish sauce at Asian markets, online, and in some grocery stores in the Asian or international section. Fish sauce has a pungent aroma and a rich, salty flavor that enhances the beef.

- **Hands-On Time: 25 minutes**
- **Cook Time: 30 minutes**

Serves 6

2 pounds beef stew meat, cut into 1" cubes

¼ cup lemon juice

2 tablespoons soy sauce

1 teaspoon ground black pepper

3 tablespoons vegetable oil

3 cloves garlic, peeled and minced

2 medium carrots, peeled and sliced

1 medium yellow onion, peeled and roughly chopped

1 medium red bell pepper, seeded and chopped

1 cup tomato sauce

2 large russet potatoes, peeled and cut into ½" cubes

1 bay leaf

3 cups Beef Stock (see recipe in Chapter 2)

1 cup water

1 In a zip-top bag or airtight storage container, add beef, lemon juice, soy sauce, and black pepper. Turn to coat beef cubes evenly, then let stand for 20 minutes. Strain off marinade and reserve. Pat beef dry.

2 Press the Sauté button on the Instant Pot® and heat oil. Add half the beef to pot in an even layer, making sure there is space between beef cubes to prevent steam from forming. Brown 3 minutes on each side. Remove from pot and reserve on a plate. Repeat with remaining beef.

3 Add garlic, carrots, onion, and bell pepper to pot and cook for 3 minutes, until just tender. Press the Cancel button. Add beef along with marinade to pot, then add remaining ingredients. Close lid, set steam release to Sealing, press the Manual button, and adjust cook time to 30 minutes.

4 When the timer beeps, let pressure release naturally, about 20 minutes. Press the Cancel button, open lid, discard bay leaf, and stir well. If you prefer a thicker stew, press the Sauté button and let stew reduce to desired thickness. Serve hot.

PER SERVING

CALORIES: 396 | FAT: 15g | PROTEIN: 38g | SODIUM: 375mg
FIBER: 5g | CARBOHYDRATES: 30g | SUGAR: 5g

9

Chilis

When you think of chili, what comes to mind? Depending on where you're from your idea of chili might be quite different than someone else's. Chili originated in the area that is now northern Mexico and southern Texas, where it was a popular dish with workers. Its popularity grew, and by the early 1900s chili began to spread across the United States, and different regions added their own spin to the dish.

In Texas, chili is chunks of beef cooked with chilies and definitely has no beans. In Cincinnati, it is a beefy mixture reimagined by Greek immigrants and is often served over spaghetti and flavored with chocolate. In the Southwest, chili is often green due to the types of chilies used to flavor the dish. While chili may be different across the country, there is one thing all different types of chili have in common. The Instant Pot® will make chili making fast, easy, and incredibly flavorful!

Cooking chili under pressure will help infuse all the ingredients with flavor. Meats and vegetables will be perfectly tender, beans will stay plump, and it all will be ready to eat in about an hour. Compared to 3–4 hours on the stove for some types of chili, that is a tremendous amount of time saved.

Traditional Beef Chili

If you can't find chili meat in your grocery store, you can ask the butcher to grind some for you. For the best flavor you should use a fattier cut of meat, like chuck or short rib. This chili does not include beans, but feel free to stir in a can of rinsed and drained red beans after it has finished cooking.

- **Hands-On Time: 25 minutes**
- **Cook Time: 35 minutes**

Serves 8

2 pounds chili meat made from chuck roast

1 medium onion, peeled and chopped

3 cloves garlic, peeled and minced

¼ cup chili powder

1 teaspoon ground cumin

2 tablespoons light brown sugar

½ teaspoon salt

½ teaspoon ground black pepper

2 cups Beef Broth (see recipe in Chapter 2)

2½ cups water, divided

¼ cup corn masa

1 tablespoon lime juice

1 Press the Sauté button on the Instant Pot® and brown meat well, about 10 minutes. Add onion, garlic, chili powder, cumin, brown sugar, salt, and pepper and cook until the onions are just tender, about 10 minutes.

2 Add broth and 2 cups of water and stir well. Press the Cancel button, close lid, set steam release to Sealing, press the Chili button, and cook for the default time of 30 minutes.

3 When the timer beeps, quick-release the pressure, open lid and stir well. Press the Cancel button, then press the Sauté button. Whisk together reserved water and masa and whisk into chili. Bring to a boil, stirring constantly, until it starts to thicken, about 5 minutes. Press the Cancel button, then add lime juice. Serve hot.

PER SERVING

CALORIES: 202 | FAT: 5g | PROTEIN: 27g | SODIUM: 400mg
FIBER: 2g | CARBOHYDRATES: 10g | SUGAR: 4g

Beef Chili with Beans

Adding beans to chili helps stretch a smaller amount of beef to feed more people. This chili is also more affordable since it uses regular ground beef instead of the more expensive cuts of beef ground for chili meat. The best part is that you will still have an amazing meal, and you can save a few pennies in the process!

- **Hands-On Time: 20 minutes**
- **Cook Time: 20 minutes**

Serves 8

1 pound 80% lean ground beef

1 medium onion, peeled and chopped

2 cloves garlic, peeled and minced

¼ cup chili powder

1 teaspoon ground cumin

½ teaspoon ground coriander

2 tablespoons brown sugar

½ teaspoon salt

½ teaspoon ground black pepper

1 (14.5-ounce) can diced tomatoes

2 cups dried pinto beans, soaked overnight in water to cover and drained

2 cups Beef Broth (see recipe in Chapter 2)

1 tablespoon lime juice

1 Press the Sauté button on the Instant Pot® and brown beef until no pink remains, about 10 minutes. Add onion, garlic, chili powder, cumin, coriander, brown sugar, salt, and pepper and cook until the onions are just tender, about 10 minutes.

2 Add tomatoes, soaked beans, and broth and stir well. Press the Cancel button, close lid, set steam release to Sealing, press the Manual button, and set time to 20 minutes.

3 When the timer beeps, let pressure release naturally, about 20 minutes. Press the Cancel button and open lid. Add the lime juice and stir well. Serve hot.

PER SERVING

CALORIES: 353 | FAT: 11g | PROTEIN: 21g | SODIUM: 377mg
FIBER: 9g | CARBOHYDRATES: 38g | SUGAR: 6g

Beef and Sweet Potato Chili

Tender chunks of sweet potato add a unique texture and burst of sweetness to this savory chili. To ensure the sweet potatoes cook evenly, cut them into equal-sized pieces. For this chili ¼" pieces are best. Large chunks will feel too similar to a stew, and if you make them too small they will turn into mush.

- **Hands-On Time: 20 minutes**
- **Cook Time: 15 minutes**

Serves 6

2 pounds 80% lean ground beef

1 medium onion, peeled and finely chopped

1 (14.5-ounce) can diced tomatoes, drained

3 cloves garlic, peeled and minced

¼ cup chili powder

½ teaspoon ground cumin

½ teaspoon dried oregano

½ teaspoon smoked paprika

½ teaspoon salt

½ teaspoon ground black pepper

1 (28-ounce) can crushed tomatoes

2 cups Chicken Broth (see recipe in Chapter 2)

2 medium sweet potatoes, peeled and diced

1 Press the Sauté button on the Instant Pot® and brown beef, crumbling well, until browned, about 10 minutes. Add onion and cook until tender, about 5 minutes. Add tomatoes, garlic, chili powder, cumin, oregano, paprika, salt, and pepper and cook until fragrant, about 2 minutes.

2 Add tomatoes, broth, and sweet potatoes and stir well. Press the Cancel button, close lid, set steam release to Sealing, press the Manual button, and adjust time to 15 minutes.

3 When the timer beeps, let pressure naturally release, about 20 minutes. Open lid and stir well. Serve hot.

PER SERVING

CALORIES: 512 | FAT: 27g | PROTEIN: 31g | SODIUM: 1,139mg
FIBER: 7g | CARBOHYDRATES: 28g | SUGAR: 12g

Chipotle Beer Chili

Chipotle peppers in adobo are dried, smoked jalapeños mixed with a tangy red sauce. You can find chipotle peppers in adobo in both cans and jars in the international foods section of most grocery stores. Mexican lager beers (like Corona) are ideal for this chili—the bright flavor of the beer keeps it from becoming too heavy. Serve with lime wedges and chopped white onions.

- **Hands-On Time: 25 minutes**
- **Cook Time: 35 minutes**

Serves 8

2 pounds chili meat made from chuck roast

1 medium onion, peeled and chopped

3 cloves garlic, peeled and minced

3 tablespoons minced chipotle in adobo

2 tablespoons chili powder

1 teaspoon ground cumin

½ teaspoon ground coriander

2 tablespoons light brown sugar

½ teaspoon salt

½ teaspoon ground black pepper

2 cups Beef Broth (see recipe in Chapter 2)

1 (12-ounce) bottle lager-style beer

½ cup water

¼ cup corn masa

1 tablespoon lime juice

1 Press the Sauté button on the Instant Pot® and brown chili meat well, about 10 minutes. Add onion, garlic, chipotle, chili powder, cumin, coriander, brown sugar, salt, and pepper and cook until the onions are just tender, about 10 minutes.

2 Add broth and beer and stir well. Press the Cancel button, close lid, set steam release to Sealing, press the Chili button, and cook for the default time of 30 minutes.

3 When the timer beeps, quick-release the pressure, open lid, and stir well. Press the Cancel button, then press the Sauté button. Whisk together water and masa and whisk into chili. Bring to a boil, stirring constantly, until it starts to thicken, about 5 minutes. Press the Cancel button, then add the lime juice. Serve hot.

PER SERVING

CALORIES: 209 | FAT: 5g | PROTEIN: 27g | SODIUM: 414mg
FIBER: 2g | CARBOHYDRATES: 11g | SUGAR: 5g

Texas Red Chili

The sauce for this chili is made with roasted dry chilies that are soaked and then puréed into a sauce. Dried chilies are usually available in the produce department or in the international food section of most grocery stores. Serve with sour cream and shredded cheese.

- Hands-On Time: 25 minutes
- Cook Time: 30 minutes, plus 40 minutes for preparing chilies

Serves 8

2 dried Anaheim chilies, halved and seeded

2 dried New Mexico chilies, halved and seeded

1 tablespoon chili powder

1 teaspoon ground cumin

1 (12-ounce) can lager- or bock-style beer, divided

1 tablespoon vegetable oil

2 pounds chili meat made from chuck roast

1 medium onion, peeled and chopped

2 cloves garlic, peeled and minced

1 tablespoon light brown sugar

½ teaspoon salt

½ teaspoon ground black pepper

2 cups Beef Broth (see recipe in Chapter 2)

1½ cups water, divided

¼ cup corn masa

1 tablespoon lime juice

1 teaspoon hot sauce

1 Heat the oven to 350°F.

2 Place chilies on a baking sheet and roast for 8 minutes. Place chilies in a large heatproof bowl and cover with hot water. Let chilies soak until tender, about 30 minutes.

3 Drain chilies and place in a blender with chili powder, cumin, and half the beer. Purée until smooth, about 1 minute. Set aside.

4 Press the Sauté button on the Instant Pot® and heat oil. Add chili meat and brown, stirring often, about 8 minutes. Add onion, garlic, brown sugar, salt, and pepper and cook until onions are just tender, about 10 minutes.

5 Add chili paste, broth, 1 cup water, and remaining beer. Stir well, scraping any bits from bottom of pot. Press the Cancel button. Close lid, set steam release to Sealing, press the Chili button, and cook for the default time of 30 minutes.

6 When the timer beeps, let pressure release naturally, about 20 minutes. Open lid and stir well. Press the Cancel button, then press the Sauté button.

7 In a small bowl mix masa with reserved water. Whisk mixture into the chili, then add lime juice and hot sauce. Bring chili to a boil to thicken, about 5 minutes. Serve hot.

PER SERVING

CALORIES: 220 | FAT: 7g | PROTEIN: 27g | SODIUM: 319mg
FIBER: 1g | CARBOHYDRATES: 10g | SUGAR: 4g

Cincinnati Chili

Citizens of Cincinnati are proud of their unique style of chili, usually found in chili parlors that specialize in the signature dish served in a variety of ways. This chili is served over pasta with shredded cheese, called a 3-way. Add onions for a 4-way, and add more beans for 5-way chili.

- **Hands-On Time: 15 minutes**
- **Cook Time: 10 minutes**

Serves 8

2 pounds 90% lean ground beef

3 large yellow onions, peeled and diced, divided

3 cloves garlic, peeled and minced

2 (16-ounce) cans kidney beans, rinsed and drained

1 (15-ounce) can tomato sauce

1 cup Beef Broth (see recipe in Chapter 2)

2 tablespoons chili powder

2 tablespoons semisweet chocolate chips

2 tablespoons red wine vinegar

2 tablespoons honey

1 tablespoon pumpkin pie spice

1 teaspoon ground cumin

½ teaspoon ground cardamom

¼ teaspoon ground cloves

½ teaspoon salt

½ teaspoon freshly cracked black pepper

1 pound cooked spaghetti

4 cups shredded Cheddar cheese

1. Press the Sauté button on the Instant Pot® and add ground beef and ¾ of the diced onion. Cook, stirring often, until the beef is browned and the onion is transparent, about 8 minutes. Drain off and discard any excess fat. Add garlic and cook for 30 seconds.

2. Add beans, tomato sauce, broth, chili powder, chocolate chips, vinegar, honey, pumpkin pie spice, cumin, cardamom, cloves, salt, and pepper and mix well, then cook for 1 minute or until fragrant.

3. Press the Cancel button, close lid, set steam release to Sealing, press the Manual button, and adjust cook time to 10 minutes. When the timer beeps, quick-release the pressure and open lid. Stir well. Serve over spaghetti and top with reserved onions and cheese.

PER SERVING

CALORIES: 633 | **FAT:** 25g | **PROTEIN:** 47g | **SODIUM:** 1,059mg
FIBER: 9g | **CARBOHYDRATES:** 48g | **SUGAR:** 10g

Buffalo Chicken Chili

This chili has the spicy, zippy flavor of buffalo wings made into a creamy chili. Use any buffalo wing sauce you prefer—as spicy or as mild as you like. If you want to make this dish look extra fancy, top each bowl with crumbled blue cheese and small pieces of diced celery.

- **Hands-On Time: 15 minutes**
- **Cook Time: 32 minutes**

Serves 6

1 tablespoon vegetable oil

1 medium onion, peeled and chopped

1 stalk celery, finely chopped

2 cloves garlic, peeled and minced

½ cup Buffalo-style hot sauce

½ teaspoon salt

½ teaspoon ground black pepper

1 (15-ounce) can fire-roasted tomatoes, drained

2 (15-ounce) cans cannellini beans, drained and rinsed

2 cups Chicken Broth (see recipe in Chapter 2)

3 (6-ounce) bone-in chicken breasts, skin removed

8 ounces cream cheese, cubed, at room temperature

1 cup shredded Monterey jack cheese

¼ cup sliced scallions

1 Press the Sauté button on the Instant Pot® and heat oil. Add onion, celery, and garlic and cook until the onions are just tender, about 5 minutes.

2 Add hot sauce, salt, pepper, tomatoes, and beans and stir well. Add broth and chicken breasts. Press the Cancel button, close lid, set steam release to Sealing, press the Manual button, and set time to 30 minutes.

3 When the timer beeps, let pressure release naturally, about 20 minutes. Press the Cancel button and open lid. Carefully remove chicken, remove meat from bones, and shred with two forks. Set aside.

4 Press the Sauté button. Add cream cheese and mix until thoroughly melted. Add chicken and shredded cheese and cook until cheese is melted and smooth, about 2 minutes. Press the Cancel button. Serve hot with scallions for garnish.

PER SERVING

CALORIES: 433 | **FAT:** 20g | **PROTEIN:** 31g | **SODIUM:** 1,464mg
FIBER: 10g | **CARBOHYDRATES:** 29g | **SUGAR:** 4g

Cheesy Macaroni and Chili

Chili mac is a popular meal with adults and children alike. It's creamy, cheesy, and very satisfying. It is also full of vegetables, so if you have any picky eaters in the family, you may find this recipe is an excellent way to sneak in a few extra vegetables. For a vegetarian chili mac, substitute meat-flavored soy crumbles or crumbled tofu for the beef and Roasted Vegetable Stock (see recipe in Chapter 2) for the broth.

- **Hands-On Time: 25 minutes**
- **Cook Time: 34 minutes**

Serves 8

1 pound chili meat made from chuck roast

1 medium onion, peeled and finely chopped

1 medium red bell pepper, seeded and finely chopped

1 medium carrot, peeled and finely chopped

1 (15-ounce) can fire-roasted tomatoes, drained

3 cloves garlic, peeled and minced

2 tablespoons chili powder

1 teaspoon ground cumin

½ teaspoon dried oregano

½ teaspoon salt

½ teaspoon ground black pepper

2 cups Beef Broth (see recipe in Chapter 2)

6 ounces elbow macaroni

4 ounces cream cheese

¼ cup heavy cream

1½ cups shredded mild Cheddar cheese

1 Press the Sauté button on the Instant Pot® and brown chili meat well, about 10 minutes. Once browned add onion, bell pepper, and carrot. Cook until the vegetables are tender, about 8 minutes. Add tomatoes, garlic, chili powder, cumin, oregano, salt, and black pepper and cook until fragrant, about 2 minutes.

2 Add broth and stir well. Press the Cancel button, close lid, set steam release to Sealing, press the Chili button, and cook for the default time of 30 minutes.

3 When the timer beeps, quick-release the pressure, open lid, and stir well. Press the Cancel button, then stir in macaroni. Close lid, set steam release to Sealing, press the Manual button, and adjust time to 4 minutes. When the timer beeps, quick-release the pressure. Open lid and stir well. Add cream cheese and stir until melted. Add cream and Cheddar cheese and stir until cheese is completely melted. Serve hot.

PER SERVING

CALORIES: 355 | FAT: 16g | PROTEIN: 23g | SODIUM: 602mg
FIBER: 3g | CARBOHYDRATES: 24g | SUGAR: 4g

Vegan Chili

Finely chopped vegetables combined with bulgur wheat give this chili a satisfying texture and flavor. If you choose to use canned beans in place of dried, you can add three cans of drained and rinsed beans after cooking is complete. Let the chili sit on the Keep Warm setting for 10 minutes before serving to heat the canned beans through.

- **Hands-On Time: 10 minutes**
- **Cook Time: 30 minutes**

Serves 8

1 tablespoon olive oil

2 medium white onions, peeled and finely chopped

1 medium red bell pepper, seeded and finely chopped

1 medium carrot, peeled and finely chopped

2 small jalapeño peppers, seeded and finely chopped

2 cloves garlic, minced

1 (28-ounce) can diced tomatoes

1 (15-ounce) can tomato sauce

¼ cup chili powder

¼ cup chopped cilantro

1 tablespoon smoked paprika

1½ teaspoons ground cumin

1 teaspoon ground coriander

½ teaspoon salt

½ teaspoon black pepper

2 cups dried kidney beans, soaked overnight in water to cover and drained

½ cup bulgur wheat

3 cups Vegetable Broth (see recipe in Chapter 2)

1 cup water

1 Press the Sauté button on the Instant Pot® and heat oil. Add onions, bell pepper, and carrot and sauté until vegetables are tender, about 8 minutes. Add jalapeños and garlic and cook until fragrant, about 1 minute. Press the Cancel button.

2 Place tomatoes, tomato sauce, chili powder, cilantro, paprika, cumin, coriander, salt, black pepper, beans, bulgur, broth, and water in pot. Close lid, set steam release to Sealing, press the Chili button, and cook for the default time of 30 minutes.

3 When the timer beeps, quick-release the pressure, open lid, and stir well. If chili is too thin, press the Cancel button and then press the Sauté button and let chili simmer, uncovered, until desired thickness is reached. Serve warm.

PER SERVING

CALORIES: 281 | **FAT:** 4g | **PROTEIN:** 14g | **SODIUM:** 708mg
FIBER: 14g | **CARBOHYDRATES:** 50g | **SUGAR:** 8g

Black Bean and Corn Chili

This chili is a good balance between lean meat, sweet corn, and earthy black beans. It actually tastes better with time, making it an excellent candidate for your weekly meal prep rotation! If fresh corn is in season and available in your local market, you can substitute it here. Two or three large cobs should yield 1 cup of corn kernels.

- **Hands-On Time: 10 minutes**
- **Cook Time: 30 minutes**

Serves 8

1 tablespoon vegetable oil

1 medium white onion, peeled and chopped

1 medium red bell pepper, seeded and chopped

1 medium carrot, peeled and chopped

½ pound ground turkey

1½ cups dried black beans, soaked overnight in water to cover and drained

1 cup frozen corn kernels

1 (28-ounce) can diced tomatoes

3 tablespoons chili powder

1 tablespoon smoked paprika

2 teaspoons ground cumin

1 teaspoon ground coriander

½ teaspoon salt

½ teaspoon ground black pepper

3 cups Vegetable Broth (see recipe in Chapter 2)

1 cup water

1 Press the Sauté button on the Instant Pot® and heat oil. Add onion, bell pepper, and carrot and cook until softened, about 5 minutes. Add ground turkey and cook until turkey is no longer pink, about 6 minutes. Press the Cancel button.

2 Place remaining ingredients in pot. Close lid, set steam release to Sealing, press the Chili button, and cook for the default time of 30 minutes.

3 When the timer beeps, quick-release the pressure, open lid, and stir well. If chili is too thin, press the Cancel button and then press the Sauté button and let chili simmer, uncovered, until desired thickness is reached. Serve warm.

PER SERVING

CALORIES: 248 | FAT: 6g | PROTEIN: 15g | SODIUM: 443mg
FIBER: 10g | CARBOHYDRATES: 36g | SUGAR: 6g

Black Bean Chili with Quinoa

Quinoa adds a pleasant nutty flavor to this chili. It is ideal for those looking to incorporate more plant-based recipes in their diet. The black beans in this recipe are an excellent source of dietary fiber, and are well known for being heart healthy.

- **Hands-On Time: 10 minutes**
- **Cook Time: 10 minutes**

Serves 6

1 tablespoon vegetable oil

1 medium onion, peeled and chopped

1 medium red bell pepper, seeded and chopped

2 cloves garlic, peeled and minced

3 tablespoons chili powder

1 teaspoon ground cumin

½ teaspoon salt

½ teaspoon ground black pepper

2 cups Vegetable Broth (see recipe in Chapter 2)

1 cup water

¾ cup quinoa

2 (15-ounce) cans black beans, drained and rinsed

1 Press the Sauté button on the Instant Pot® and heat oil. Add onion and bell pepper. Cook until vegetables are soft, about 5 minutes. Add garlic, chili powder, cumin, salt, and black pepper and cook until fragrant, about 1 minute.

2 Add broth and water and stir well, then add quinoa and beans. Press the Cancel button, close lid, set steam release to Sealing, press the Manual button, and adjust time to 10 minutes.

3 When the timer beeps, quick-release the pressure, open lid, and stir well. Serve hot.

PER SERVING

CALORIES: 260 | FAT: 5g | PROTEIN: 13g | SODIUM: 712mg
FIBER: 13g | CARBOHYDRATES: 43g | SUGAR: 2g

BLACK BEAN BENEFITS
Studies show that black beans can help lower blood pressure, lower cholesterol, and might even help prevent heart disease. These benefits are due to the combination of potassium, calcium, and magnesium, which can help maintain heart health. High-fiber beans may help improve blood glucose levels as well.

Three-Bean Vegetarian Chili

This chili is packed with nutrition, but is low in fat. It will fill you up and keep you full for a long time, and you can enjoy it without any guilt. While the recipe calls for three types of beans for a fun texture, taste, and visual appeal, you can make it with any beans you like.

- **Hands-On Time: 5 minutes**
- **Cook Time: 30 minutes**

Serves 8

1 cup dried pinto beans, soaked overnight in water to cover and drained

1 cup dried red beans, soaked overnight in water to cover and drained

1 cup dried black beans, soaked overnight in water to cover and drained

2 medium white onions, peeled and chopped

2 medium red bell peppers, seeded and chopped

2 stalks celery, chopped

1 (28-ounce) can diced tomatoes

1 (15-ounce) can tomato sauce

¼ cup chili powder

2 tablespoons smoked paprika

1 teaspoon ground cumin

1 teaspoon ground coriander

½ teaspoon salt

½ teaspoon ground black pepper

3 cups Vegetable Broth (see recipe in Chapter 2)

1 cup water

1 Place all ingredients in the Instant Pot®. Close lid, set steam release to Sealing, press the Chili button, and cook for the default time of 30 minutes.

2 When the timer beeps, quick-release the pressure, open lid, and stir well. If chili is too thin, press the Cancel button and then press the Sauté button and let chili simmer, uncovered, until desired thickness is reached. Serve warm.

PER SERVING

CALORIES: 323 | **FAT:** 2g | **PROTEIN:** 18g | **SODIUM:** 712mg
FIBER: 17g | **CARBOHYDRATES:** 60g | **SUGAR:** 9g

Venison Chili

Venison has a savory, rich flavor, but it is lower in cholesterol, fat, and calories than similar cuts of beef and pork. It's a smarter choice when you are trying to stick to a heart-healthy diet while still enjoying foods you love.

- **Hands-On Time: 20 minutes**
- **Cook Time: 30 minutes**

Serves 8

2 pounds ground venison

1 medium yellow onion, peeled and chopped

1 medium poblano pepper, seeded and chopped

2 cloves garlic, peeled and minced

1 (28-ounce) can diced tomatoes

¼ cup chili powder

1 teaspoon ground cumin

1 teaspoon smoked paprika

½ teaspoon dried oregano

½ teaspoon salt

½ teaspoon ground black pepper

1 cup dried kidney beans, soaked overnight in water to cover and drained

4 cups Beef Broth (see recipe in Chapter 2)

1 teaspoon Worcestershire sauce

1 Press the Sauté button on the Instant Pot® and brown venison well, about 10 minutes. Add onion, poblano pepper, garlic, tomatoes, chili powder, cumin, paprika, oregano, salt, and black pepper and cook until the onions are just tender, about 10 minutes.

2 Add beans, broth, and Worcestershire sauce to pot and stir well. Press the Cancel button, close lid, set steam release to Sealing, press the Chili button, and cook for the default time of 30 minutes.

3 When the timer beeps, quick-release the pressure, open lid, and stir well. Serve hot.

PER SERVING

CALORIES: 273 | FAT: 4g | PROTEIN: 32g | SODIUM: 560mg
FIBER: 7g | CARBOHYDRATES: 25g | SUGAR: 4g

Turkey Chili

If you have turkey left over from the holidays or a Sunday supper, you can chop it up and use it in place of the ground turkey. Don't sauté the cooked turkey, just add it in with the liquids and cook as directed.

- **Hands-On Time: 15 minutes**
- **Cook Time: 30 minutes**

Serves 8

2 pounds ground turkey

1 medium onion, peeled and chopped

1 medium carrot, peeled and finely chopped

3 cloves garlic, peeled and minced

1 small jalapeño pepper, seeded and minced

¼ cup chili powder

1 teaspoon ground cumin

½ teaspoon smoked paprika

1 tablespoon light brown sugar

½ teaspoon salt

½ teaspoon ground black pepper

2 cups Chicken Broth (see recipe in Chapter 2)

1 cup water

1 (15-ounce) can kidney beans, drained and rinsed

1 tablespoon lime juice

1 Press the Sauté button on the Instant Pot® and brown turkey well, about 10 minutes. Add onion, carrot, garlic, jalapeño, chili powder, cumin, and paprika and cook until fragrant, about 3 minutes. Add brown sugar, salt, and pepper and cook 30 seconds.

2 Add broth and water. Stir well, then press the Cancel button, close lid, set steam release to Sealing, press the Chili button, and cook for the default time of 30 minutes.

3 When the timer beeps, quick-release the pressure, open lid, and stir well. Stir in beans and lime juice and let stand for 10 minutes to heat beans. If chili is too thin, press the Cancel button and then press the Sauté button and let chili simmer, uncovered, until desired thickness is reached. Serve warm.

PER SERVING

CALORIES: 247 | FAT: 10g | PROTEIN: 25g | SODIUM: 418mg
FIBER: 5g | CARBOHYDRATES: 14g | SUGAR: 3g

Lamb Chili

This richly spiced chili is a unique change from beef- or turkey-based chili. Lamb adds a grassy flavor that is complemented by the earthy cumin and tangy tomato. Be sure to use fattier ground lamb for this chili. Lean lamb runs the risk of becoming dry after pressure cooking. If you have leftover lamb roast, cut it into ½" chunks and use the chunks in place of the ground meat.

- **Hands-On Time: 15 minutes**
- **Cook Time: 30 minutes**

Serves 6

3 tablespoons extra-virgin olive oil

2 pounds ground lamb

1 large yellow onion, peeled and diced

4 cloves garlic, peeled and minced

2 tablespoons chili powder

1 tablespoon ground cumin

½ teaspoon oregano

2 small jalapeño peppers, seeded and minced

2 medium green bell peppers, seeded and diced

1 (28-ounce) can diced tomatoes

1 (8-ounce) can tomato sauce

1 teaspoon Worcestershire sauce

1 cup dried white beans, soaked overnight in water to cover and drained

½ teaspoon salt

½ teaspoon freshly cracked black pepper

1 Press the Sauté button on the Instant Pot® and heat oil. Add lamb, onion, garlic, chili powder, and cumin to pot. Cook, crumbling lamb meat, until meat is brown and onion is transparent, about 8 minutes. Add oregano, jalapeños, and bell peppers and cook until bell pepper is just tender, about 5 minutes. Press the Cancel button.

2 Add tomatoes, tomato sauce, Worcestershire sauce, beans, salt, and black pepper. Stir well, close lid, set steam release to Sealing, press the Chili button, and cook for the default time of 30 minutes. When the timer beeps, let pressure release naturally, about 20 minutes. Open lid and stir well. Serve hot.

PER SERVING

CALORIES: 671 | FAT: 40g | PROTEIN: 36g | SODIUM: 797mg
FIBER: 10g | CARBOHYDRATES: 36g | SUGAR: 8g

Chicken and White Bean Chili

This chili is excellent alone, but you can also use it for a delicious chicken casserole. In a 9" x 13" casserole dish, layer 3 cups of the chili between three layers of 4 corn tortillas each, and sprinkle ½ cup shredded jack cheese per layer. Top with additional cheese and bake at 350°F for 25–30 minutes or until the casserole is hot throughout and cheese is melted!

- **Hands-On Time: 20 minutes**
- **Cook Time: 30 minutes**

Serves 6

1 tablespoon vegetable oil

1 medium onion, peeled and chopped

2 cloves garlic, peeled and minced

1 tablespoon ground cumin

1 teaspoon ground coriander

½ teaspoon salt

½ teaspoon ground black pepper

2 (6-ounce) cans diced green chilies

2 cups dried white beans, soaked overnight in water to cover and drained

2 cups Chicken Broth (see recipe in Chapter 2)

3 (6-ounce) bone-in chicken breasts, skin removed

1 Press the Sauté button on the Instant Pot® and heat oil. Add onion, garlic, cumin, coriander, salt, and pepper and cook until the onions are just tender, about 10 minutes.

2 Add green chilies, beans, and broth and stir well. Add chicken breasts. Press the Cancel button, close lid, set steam release to Sealing, press the Manual button, and set time to 30 minutes.

3 When the timer beeps, let pressure release naturally, about 20 minutes. Open lid. Carefully remove chicken, remove meat from bones, and shred with two forks. Set aside.

4 Remove 1 cup of beans and liquid from the pot and mash with a potato masher or purée in a food processor. Stir chicken and mashed beans into pot. Serve hot.

PER SERVING

CALORIES: 365 | FAT: 4g | PROTEIN: 33g | SODIUM: 430mg
FIBER: 13g | CARBOHYDRATES: 47g | SUGAR: 4g

Green Chicken Chili

The green color in this chili comes from the combination of poblano and Anaheim peppers, along with tomatillos. This combination results in a fresh, light-flavored chili. To dress it up, serve it with crushed corn chips, a mild white cheese such as queso quesadilla, chopped fresh cilantro, and sour cream as garnishes.

- **Hands-On Time: 15 minutes**
- **Cook Time: 30 minutes**

Serves 8

2 tablespoons unsalted butter

1 medium yellow onion, peeled and chopped

½ pound poblano peppers, seeded and roughly chopped

½ pound Anaheim peppers, seeded and roughly chopped

½ pound tomatillos, husked and quartered

2 small jalapeño peppers, seeded and roughly chopped

2 cloves garlic, peeled and minced

1 teaspoon ground cumin

6 bone-in, skin-on chicken thighs (2½ pounds total)

2 cups Chicken Stock (see recipe in Chapter 2)

2 cups water

⅓ cup roughly chopped fresh cilantro

3 (15-ounce) cans Great Northern beans, drained and rinsed

1 Press the Sauté button on the Instant Pot® and melt butter. Add onion and cook until softened, about 3 minutes. Add poblano and Anaheim peppers, tomatillos, and jalapeños and cook 3 minutes, then add garlic and cumin and cook until fragrant, about 30 seconds. Press the Cancel button.

2 Add chicken thighs, stock, and water to pot. Close lid, set steam release to Sealing, press the Chili button, and cook for the default time of 30 minutes.

3 When the timer beeps, quick-release the pressure, open lid, and stir well. Press the Cancel button and remove chicken to a cutting board. Carefully remove skin from chicken and shred meat with two forks.

4 Use an immersion blender to purée sauce until smooth. Stir meat, cilantro, and beans into sauce. Serve warm.

PER SERVING

CALORIES: 304 | FAT: 10g | PROTEIN: 33g | SODIUM: 154mg
FIBER: 7g | CARBOHYDRATES: 19g | SUGAR: 3g

Black-Eyed Pea Chili with Pork

This chunky chili features two ingredients that are made for each other. Black-eyed peas and pork are a traditional combination in the southern part of the United States, and for good reason. Fatty pork complements the starchy, almost potato-like flavor of black-eyed peas. Make this chili as a substitute for traditional Hoppin' John served on New Year's Day to usher in good luck and prosperity. It can't hurt to start the year off with a delicious meal!

- **Hands-On Time: 30 minutes**
- **Cook Time: 30 minutes**

Serves 6

2 tablespoons vegetable oil

2 pounds boneless pork shoulder, cut into 1" pieces

1 medium onion, peeled and finely chopped

1 (14.5-ounce) can diced tomatoes, drained

3 cloves garlic, peeled and minced

3 tablespoons chili powder

1 teaspoon ground cumin

½ teaspoon ground coriander

½ teaspoon salt

½ teaspoon ground black pepper

4 cups Chicken Broth (see recipe in Chapter 2)

2 cups dried black-eyed peas, soaked overnight in water to cover and drained

1 tablespoon lime juice

1 Press the Sauté button on the Instant Pot® and heat oil. Add half the pork to pot in an even layer, working in batches to prevent meat from steaming. Brown for 3 minutes per side. Transfer pork to a plate and reserve while you repeat with remaining pork.

2 To pot add onion and cook until tender, about 5 minutes. Add tomatoes, garlic, chili powder, cumin, coriander, salt, and pepper and cook until fragrant, about 2 minutes.

3 Add broth, black-eyed peas, and browned pork and stir well. Press the Cancel button, close lid, set steam release to Sealing, press the Manual button, and adjust time to 30 minutes.

4 When the timer beeps, let pressure naturally release, about 20 minutes. Open lid and stir in lime juice. Serve hot.

PER SERVING

CALORIES: 311 | **FAT:** 11g | **PROTEIN:** 35g | **SODIUM:** 576mg
FIBER: 5g | **CARBOHYDRATES:** 16g | **SUGAR:** 4g

New Family Favorites

Soup can be a blank canvas, allowing you to build flavors and textures to make just about anything you want it to be. The soups in this chapter are based on family-favorite meals. From dips and sandwiches to pizza and casseroles, these recipes incorporate ingredients and flavors to make delicious soups with unexpected but familiar flavors.

Using the Instant Pot®, you can create these unusual soups in record time. French Dip Soup is ready in 30 minutes, for example, but it has the savory flavor of a pot roast that has been simmering all day. Macaroni and Cheese Soup is cheesy from the inside out and is ready in a snap.

So next time you want pizza, enchilada, or cheeseburgers, consider having them in soup form. They are just as flavorful and hearty as the originals, but with the added comfort that only a big pot of homemade soup can provide.

Lasagna Soup

Enjoy all the best flavors of lasagna in a soup that is ready in no time. For extra flavor, stir a teaspoon of Italian seasoning into the ricotta used for the topping and sprinkle the soup with grated Parmesan cheese before serving.

- **Hands-On Time: 15 minutes**
- **Cook Time: 4 minutes**

Serves 8

1 pound bulk Italian sausage

1 medium onion, peeled and diced

2 cloves garlic, peeled and minced

1 teaspoon Italian seasoning

¼ teaspoon crushed red pepper flakes

1 (28-ounce) jar marinara sauce

1 (15-ounce) can crushed tomatoes

1 cup water

10 lasagna noodles, broken into 2" pieces

½ cup heavy cream

1 cup shredded mozzarella cheese

½ cup whole-milk ricotta cheese

1 Press the Sauté button on the Instant Pot® and add sausage. Cook, crumbling, until browned, about 8 minutes. Add onion and cook until tender, about 3 minutes, then add garlic, Italian seasoning, and red pepper flakes and cook for 30 seconds. Press the Cancel button.

2 Add marinara, tomatoes, water, and noodles. Close lid, set steam release to Sealing, press the Manual button, and set time to 4 minutes.

3 When the timer beeps, quick-release the pressure and open lid. Stir soup, then add cream. Ladle into bowls and top with mozzarella and ricotta cheese.

PER SERVING

CALORIES: 467 | **FAT:** 29g | **PROTEIN:** 19g | **SODIUM:** 1,037mg
FIBER: 4g | **CARBOHYDRATES:** 30g | **SUGAR:** 9g

Pasta and Meatballs Soup

Use any type of pasta you like for this fun and comforting soup, but it retains more of the classic appeal if you break up spaghetti into small pieces.

- **Hands-On Time: 45 minutes**
- **Cook Time: 24 minutes**

Serves 6

1 pound 80% lean ground beef

2 medium onions, peeled and chopped, divided

4 cloves garlic, peeled and minced, divided

1 teaspoon ground fennel, divided

¾ teaspoon salt, divided

¾ teaspoon ground black pepper, divided

¼ teaspoon crushed red pepper flakes

¼ cup bread crumbs

1 large egg, beaten

3 tablespoons vegetable oil

4 tablespoons salted butter

1 (28-ounce) can crushed tomatoes

2 cups Chicken Stock (see recipe in Chapter 2)

6 ounces spaghetti noodles, broken into 2" pieces

½ cup grated Parmesan cheese

1 In a large bowl combine ground beef, half of chopped onion, half of minced garlic, ½ teaspoon fennel, ¼ teaspoon salt, ¼ teaspoon pepper, and red pepper flakes. Gently mix to combine, then add bread crumbs and egg and mix well. Roll mixture into ½" balls. Cover and refrigerate for 1 hour.

2 Press the Sauté button on the Instant Pot® and heat oil. Add half the meatballs to pot in one layer, making sure there is space between meatballs. Cook for 3 minutes per side, until browned. Transfer meatballs to a plate and repeat with remaining meatballs.

3 Add remaining onion to pot and sauté until tender, about 5 minutes. Add remaining garlic, remaining ½ teaspoon fennel, and remaining ½ teaspoon each salt and pepper and cook for 30 seconds. Add butter and allow to melt, about 1 minute, then add tomatoes and mix well. Press the Cancel button.

4 Add meatballs and stock to pot. Close lid, set steam release to Sealing, press the Manual button, and adjust time to 20 minutes.

5 When the timer beeps, let pressure release naturally, about 20 minutes. Press the Cancel button, open lid, and stir in pasta. Close lid, set steam release to Sealing, press the Manual button, and adjust time to 4 minutes. When the timer beeps, quick-release the pressure. Top with cheese and serve hot.

PER SERVING

CALORIES: 559 | FAT: 30g | PROTEIN: 24g | SODIUM: 788mg
FIBER: 4g | CARBOHYDRATES: 40g | SUGAR: 8g

Cheeseburger Soup

Who doesn't love a cheeseburger? This soup has all the best flavors of the classic cheeseburger, even the pickles! If you like, replace the beef with ground turkey or meat-free crumbles.

- **Hands-On Time: 20 minutes**
- **Cook Time: 15 minutes**

Serves 6

3 tablespoons vegetable oil

1 pound 80% lean ground beef

1 medium onion, peeled and chopped

2 medium tomatoes, seeded and chopped

2 cloves garlic, peeled and minced

½ teaspoon salt

½ teaspoon ground black pepper

1 large russet potato, peeled and cut into ½" cubes

3 cups Beef Stock (see recipe in Chapter 2)

1 cup heavy whipping cream

1 cup shredded American cheese

1 cup shredded Cheddar cheese

¼ cup chopped dill pickle slices

1 cup plain croutons

1 Press the Sauté button on the Instant Pot® and heat oil. Add beef to pot and cook, crumbling well, until browned, about 10 minutes. Add onion and tomatoes and cook until onion is tender, about 5 minutes. Add garlic, salt, and pepper and cook for 30 seconds.

2 Add potato and stock to pot. Stir well, then press the Cancel button. Close lid, set steam release to Sealing, press the Manual button, and adjust cook time to 15 minutes.

3 When the timer beeps, let pressure release naturally, about 20 minutes. Press the Cancel button, open lid, and stir in cream. Add cheese ½ cup at a time, making sure the cheese has melted completely before adding more. Serve hot, topped with dill pickles and croutons.

PER SERVING

CALORIES: 655 | FAT: 45g | PROTEIN: 28g | SODIUM: 981mg
FIBER: 2g | CARBOHYDRATES: 25g | SUGAR: 6g

Chicken Potpie Soup

If you want a true pastry top for your bowls instead of the crackers, you can buy puff pastry dough or ready-made pie crust. Roll the dough out on a floured board and use a soup bowl as a template to cut out circles. Bake as directed and place them on your filled soup bowls.

- **Hands-On Time: 15 minutes**
- **Cook Time: 15 minutes**

Serves 6

3 tablespoons vegetable oil

2 stalks celery, chopped

1 medium onion, peeled and chopped

1 medium carrot, peeled and chopped

2 cloves garlic, peeled and minced

½ teaspoon salt

½ teaspoon ground black pepper

¼ teaspoon dried thyme

3 tablespoons all-purpose flour

3 cups Chicken Stock (see recipe in Chapter 2)

3 cups shredded cooked chicken breast

½ cup heavy whipping cream

1 cup frozen peas

12 round butter crackers, such as Ritz

1 Press the Sauté button on the Instant Pot® and heat oil. Add celery, onion, and carrot and cook until tender, about 8 minutes. Add garlic, salt, pepper, and thyme and cook until fragrant, about 30 seconds.

2 Sprinkle flour over vegetables and cook, stirring well, until flour is completely moistened, about 1 minute. Slowly whisk in stock, making sure to scrape any bits off the bottom of the pot. Press the Cancel button and stir in chicken. Close lid, set steam release to Sealing, press the Manual button, and adjust cook time to 5 minutes.

3 When the timer beeps, quick-release the pressure. Open lid, stir soup well, and stir in cream and peas. Let stand on the Keep Warm setting for 10 minutes, or until peas are hot and tender. Ladle into bowls and top each bowl with 2 crackers. Serve immediately.

PER SERVING

CALORIES: 334 | FAT: 18g | PROTEIN: 26g | SODIUM: 257mg
FIBER: 2g | CARBOHYDRATES: 14g | SUGAR: 4g

Macaroni and Cheese Soup

If you are serving this soup to picky eaters, you may want to purée the vegetables into the broth to disguise them. Once the first round of cooking is complete, use an immersion blender or a regular blender to purée the soup until smooth.

- **Hands-On Time: 15 minutes**
- **Cook Time: 9 minutes**

Serves 8

3 tablespoons unsalted butter

2 medium carrots, peeled and finely chopped

2 stalks celery, diced

1 medium onion, peeled and diced

1 clove garlic, minced

1 teaspoon dried mustard

3 cups Chicken Broth (see recipe in Chapter 2)

8 ounces elbow macaroni

1 cup heavy cream

2 cups shredded sharp Cheddar cheese

1 cup shredded American cheese

WHY AMERICAN CHEESE?

American cheese is a combination of Cheddar, Colby, or washed cheese curds. It helps to keep sauces smooth and creamy, and makes the perfect grilled cheese sandwich. In soups, it combines with other cheeses to stay smooth. It may not be the fanciest cheese, but it's a culinary star in its own special way.

1 Press the Sauté button on the Instant Pot® and melt butter. Add carrots, celery, and onion. Cook, stirring often, until softened, about 5 minutes. Add garlic and cook until fragrant, about 30 seconds, then add mustard and stir well. Add broth, then press the Cancel button.

2 Close lid, set steam release to Sealing, press the Manual button, and set time to 5 minutes. When the timer beeps, let pressure release naturally, about 15 minutes. Press the Cancel button, open lid, and stir in pasta. Close lid, set steam release to Sealing, press the Manual button, and set time to 4 minutes.

3 When the timer beeps, quick-release the pressure. Open lid and stir soup well. Stir in cream, then stir in cheese 1 cup at a time, stirring each addition until completely melted before adding another. Serve hot.

PER SERVING

CALORIES: 450 | FAT: 27g | PROTEIN: 17g | SODIUM: 593mg
FIBER: 2g | CARBOHYDRATES: 29g | SUGAR: 5g

Unstuffed Cabbage Soup

Stuffed cabbage is delicious, but requires a lot of time and effort to make. It's much easier to toss all the same ingredients into a flavorful—and quick—soup. If you like, replace half the ground beef with ground pork. Garnish the bowls of soup with sour cream and snipped fresh dill.

- **Hands-On Time: 15 minutes**
- **Cook Time: 15 minutes**

Serves 8

2 tablespoons vegetable oil

1 pound 80% lean ground beef

1 medium yellow onion, peeled and chopped

1 medium carrot, peeled and chopped

1 large head cabbage, cored and chopped

3 cloves garlic, peeled and minced

1 tablespoon light brown sugar

4 cups Chicken Broth (see recipe in Chapter 2)

1 (29-ounce) can tomato sauce

1 bay leaf

1 teaspoon dried oregano

½ teaspoon paprika

¼ teaspoon crushed red pepper flakes

½ teaspoon salt

½ teaspoon ground black pepper

½ cup uncooked white rice

1 Press the Sauté button on the Instant Pot® and heat oil. Add ground beef and cook until just starting to brown around the edges, about 8 minutes. Add onion and carrot and cook until tender, about 5 minutes. Add cabbage and garlic and cook until fragrant, about 1 minute. Press the Cancel button.

2 Add remaining ingredients and stir well. Close lid, set steam release to Sealing, press the Manual button, and set time to 15 minutes.

3 When the timer beeps, let pressure release naturally, about 20 minutes. Discard bay leaf. Serve hot.

PER SERVING

CALORIES: 310 | FAT: 14g | PROTEIN: 15g | SODIUM: 707mg
FIBER: 6g | CARBOHYDRATES: 29g | SUGAR: 11g

Chili Dog Soup

Chili dogs are simple, but oh-so good! In this unconstructed version, a spicy chili is cooked with chunks of all-beef hot dog and topped with cheese and crisp onions for a tasty treat. If you miss the bun, serve the soup with toasted soft bread rolls for dipping.

- **Hands-On Time: 20 minutes**
- **Cook Time: 20 minutes**

Serves 8

1 pound 80% lean ground beef

1 medium white onion, peeled and chopped

2 cloves garlic, peeled and minced

¼ cup chili powder

1 teaspoon ground cumin

½ teaspoon ground coriander

2 tablespoons light brown sugar

½ teaspoon salt

½ teaspoon ground black pepper

1 (14.5-ounce) can diced tomatoes

2 cups Beef Broth (see recipe in Chapter 2)

8 all-beef hot dogs, chopped

1 cup shredded Cheddar cheese

½ cup finely chopped Vidalia onion

1 Press the Sauté button on the Instant Pot® and brown ground beef until no pink remains, about 10 minutes. Add white onion, garlic, chili powder, cumin, coriander, brown sugar, salt, and pepper and cook until the onions are just tender, about 10 minutes.

2 Add tomatoes, broth, and hot dogs and stir well. Press the Cancel button, close lid, set steam release to Sealing, press the Manual button, and set time to 20 minutes.

3 When the timer beeps, let pressure release naturally, about 20 minutes. Open lid and stir well. Serve hot with cheese and Vidalia onion for garnish.

PER SERVING

CALORIES: 404 | FAT: 28g | PROTEIN: 20g | SODIUM: 999mg
FIBER: 3g | CARBOHYDRATES: 12g | SUGAR: 7g

King Ranch Chicken Soup

No one truly knows the origins of King Ranch Chicken. Some believe it was invented on the King Ranch in south Texas, but the inhabitants have never laid claim to the recipe. Here the Tex-Mex casserole classic is made into a soup nice enough for company, but easy enough for any night of the week.

- **Hands-On Time: 20 minutes**
- **Cook Time: 5 minutes**

Serves 6

4 tablespoons salted butter

1 medium onion, peeled and chopped

1 small jalapeño pepper, seeded and chopped

2 cloves garlic, peeled and minced

1 tablespoon chili powder

½ teaspoon salt

½ teaspoon ground black pepper

3 tablespoons all-purpose flour

3 cups Chicken Stock (see recipe in Chapter 2)

1 (10-ounce) can diced tomatoes with green chilies

3 cups shredded cooked chicken breast

½ cup heavy whipping cream

2 cups shredded Cheddar cheese

¼ cup chopped fresh cilantro

3 ounces tortilla chips

1 Press the Sauté button on the Instant Pot® and melt butter. Add onion, jalapeño, and garlic and cook until tender, about 8 minutes. Add chili powder, salt, and pepper and cook until fragrant, about 30 seconds.

2 Sprinkle flour over vegetables and cook, stirring well, until flour is completely moistened, about 1 minute. Slowly whisk in stock, making sure to scrape any bits off the bottom of the pot. Press the Cancel button and stir in tomatoes and chicken. Close lid, set steam release to Sealing, press the Manual button, and adjust cook time to 5 minutes.

3 When the timer beeps, quick-release the pressure. Open lid and stir soup well, then stir in cream. Add cheese ½ cup at a time, allowing the first addition to melt before adding the next. Serve hot with cilantro and tortilla chips for garnish.

PER SERVING

CALORIES: 521 | FAT: 31g | PROTEIN: 34g | SODIUM: 786mg
FIBER: 2g | CARBOHYDRATES: 18g | SUGAR: 3g

Supreme Pizza Soup

Pizza soup is nearly as easy as takeout, and ready in less time than it takes the delivery driver to arrive at your door. Use any pizza toppings you like; just be sure to sauté any vegetables to ensure they are tender.

- **Hands-On Time: 20 minutes**
- **Cook Time: 10 minutes**

Serves 8

½ pound bulk Italian sausage

½ pound 80% lean ground beef

1 medium onion, peeled and diced

1 medium green bell pepper, seeded and chopped

1 medium red bell pepper, seeded and chopped

2 cloves garlic, peeled and minced

1 teaspoon Italian seasoning

½ teaspoon ground fennel

1 (28-ounce) jar marinara sauce

1 (15-ounce) can crushed tomatoes

1 cup water

1 cup shredded mozzarella cheese

½ cup sliced black olives

½ cup mini pepperoni slices

1 Press the Sauté button on the Instant Pot® and add sausage and beef. Cook, crumbling, until browned, about 8 minutes. Add onion and bell peppers and cook until tender, about 6 minutes, then add garlic, Italian seasoning, and fennel and cook for 30 seconds. Press the Cancel button.

2 Add marinara sauce, tomatoes, and water. Close lid, set steam release to Sealing, press the Manual button, and set time to 10 minutes.

3 When the timer beeps, quick-release the pressure and open lid. Ladle into bowls and top with mozzarella, olives, and pepperoni.

PER SERVING

CALORIES: 341 | FAT: 21g | PROTEIN: 16g | SODIUM: 1,040mg
FIBER: 4g | CARBOHYDRATES: 16g | SUGAR: 10g

Pepperoni Pizza Stew

This chunky stew uses ready-made cheese ravioli that can be found refrigerated in the deli section of most grocery stores, but you can also use frozen pasta here—just add an extra minute to the cooking time. Of course, you can also use any cheese-filled, meat-filled, or vegetable-filled pasta you prefer.

- **Hands-On Time: 15 minutes**
- **Cook Time: 6 minutes**

Serves 6

2 tablespoons vegetable oil

1 medium onion, peeled and chopped

2 cups sliced button mushrooms

1 green bell pepper, seeded and chopped

2 cloves garlic, peeled and minced

1 tablespoon Italian seasoning

2 (14.5-ounce) cans diced tomatoes

2 cups Beef Stock (see recipe in Chapter 2)

¼ pound sliced pepperoni

1 (9-ounce) package refrigerated cheese ravioli

1 cup shredded mozzarella cheese

1 Press the Sauté button on the Instant Pot® and heat oil. Add onion, mushrooms, and bell pepper and cook until vegetables are tender, about 8 minutes. Add garlic and Italian seasoning and cook until fragrant, about 30 seconds.

2 Add tomatoes, stock, and pepperoni to pot and stir well. Press the Cancel button, close lid, set steam release to Sealing, press the Manual button, and adjust cook time to 5 minutes.

3 When the timer beeps, quick-release the pressure. Press the Cancel button, open lid, stir in ravioli, close lid, set steam release to Sealing, press the Manual button, and set time to 1 minute.

4 When the timer beeps, quick-release the pressure, open lid, and stir soup. Serve hot with shredded cheese for garnish.

PER SERVING

CALORIES: 298 | **FAT:** 14g | **PROTEIN:** 13g | **SODIUM:** 876mg
FIBER: 4g | **CARBOHYDRATES:** 29g | **SUGAR:** 5g

Beef Stroganoff Soup

Traditional Beef Stroganoff is a Russian dish of beef and noodles in a sour cream–enriched sauce that is popular with young and old alike. Here the same scrumptious flavors are used for a soup that is ready in under an hour from start to finish, thanks to the Instant Pot®.

- **Hands-On Time: 25 minutes**
- **Cook Time: 11 minutes**

Serves 6

3 tablespoons salted butter

1 pound sirloin steak, thinly sliced and cut into 1" pieces

1 medium onion, peeled and chopped

4 cups sliced button mushrooms

2 cloves garlic, peeled and minced

1 tablespoon tomato paste

½ teaspoon salt

½ teaspoon ground black pepper

3 cups Beef Stock (see recipe in Chapter 2)

2 teaspoons Worcestershire sauce

1 cup dried egg noodles

½ cup sour cream

2 tablespoons all-purpose flour

¼ cup chopped fresh flat-leaf parsley

1 Press the Sauté button on the Instant Pot® and melt butter. Add beef to pot and cook, stirring often, until browned, about 10 minutes. Transfer to a plate and set aside.

2 To pot add onion and mushrooms. Cook until onions and mushrooms are tender, about 8 minutes. Add garlic, tomato paste, salt, and pepper and cook for 1 minute, or until tomato paste is slightly darker in color and fragrant.

3 Add stock and Worcestershire sauce to pot and stir well, making sure to scrape the bottom of pot to release any browned bits, then stir in noodles. Press the Cancel button, close lid, set steam release to Sealing, press the Manual button, and adjust cook time to 6 minutes.

4 When the timer beeps, let pressure release naturally, about 20 minutes. Press the Cancel button, open lid, and stir well. In a small bowl combine sour cream and flour until smooth, then add 1 cup of cooking liquid and mix well.

5 Press the Sauté button and whisk in sour cream mixture. Cook, stirring constantly, until soup is thick and bubbling, about 3 minutes. Stir in browned beef and reserved juices and cook until beef is heated through, about 2 minutes. Serve hot with parsley for garnish.

PER SERVING

CALORIES: 323 | FAT: 19g | PROTEIN: 20g | SODIUM: 343mg
FIBER: 1g | CARBOHYDRATES: 14g | SUGAR: 3g

Corned Beef Reuben Soup

One of the best things about making corned beef is the corned beef sandwiches you can make with the leftovers. You can also use that leftover corned beef for a tasty soup that borrows the best flavors from the sandwich. If you don't have a whole corned beef brisket, substitute deli-sliced corned beef.

- **Hands-On Time: 20 minutes**
- **Cook Time: 20 minutes**

Serves 6

1 tablespoon unsalted butter

1 medium yellow onion, peeled and chopped

3 cloves garlic, peeled and minced

¼ teaspoon ground fennel

¼ teaspoon salt

¼ teaspoon ground black pepper

2 tablespoons all-purpose flour

3 cups Beef Broth (see recipe in Chapter 2)

1 medium russet potato, peeled and chopped

1 pound cooked corned beef, chopped

1 cup drained sauerkraut

¼ cup heavy cream

¾ cup grated Swiss cheese

2 scallions, chopped

1 Press the Sauté button on the Instant Pot® and melt butter. Add onion and cook until tender, about 5 minutes. Add garlic, fennel, salt, and pepper and cook until fragrant, about 30 seconds. Add flour and cook, making sure flour coats the onions, about 1 minute.

2 Add broth to pot and stir well, making sure to scrape any bits off the bottom of pot. Stir in potato, corned beef, and sauerkraut and mix well. Press the Cancel button, close lid, set steam release to Sealing, press the Soup button, and cook for the default time of 20 minutes.

3 When the timer beeps, quick-release the pressure. Open lid and stir soup well. Add cream and cheese and stir until cheese is completely melted. Serve hot with scallions for garnish.

PER SERVING

CALORIES: 354 | FAT: 22g | PROTEIN: 20g | SODIUM: 1,210mg
FIBER: 2g | CARBOHYDRATES: 13g | SUGAR: 2g

Cheesy Chicken Enchilada Soup

Masa can be found in the international food section of most grocery stores, but if you can't find it you can make a flour roux on the stove instead. In a small saucepan, melt 4 tablespoons butter over medium-low heat. Whisk in ¼ cup flour and cook for 1 minute. Whisk the roux into the soup, then press the Sauté button and simmer until the soup thickens.

- **Hands-On Time: 25 minutes**
- **Cook Time: 28 minutes**

Serves 6

1 tablespoon vegetable oil

1 medium yellow onion, peeled and chopped

¼ cup chopped fresh cilantro

3 cloves garlic, peeled and minced

1 small jalapeño pepper, seeded and minced

1 (10-ounce) can diced green tomatoes with green chilies, drained

½ teaspoon ground cumin

¼ teaspoon ground coriander

¼ teaspoon salt

¼ teaspoon ground black pepper

3 cups Chicken Broth (see recipe in Chapter 2)

2 (6-ounce) boneless, skinless chicken breasts

¼ cup water

3 tablespoons masa

1 cup grated sharp Cheddar cheese

½ cup sour cream

3 ounces tortilla chips

1 Press the Sauté button on the Instant Pot® and heat oil. Add onion and cook until tender, about 5 minutes. Add cilantro, garlic, jalapeño, tomatoes, cumin, coriander, salt, and pepper and cook until fragrant, about 1 minute.

2 Add broth and chicken to pot and stir well. Press the Cancel button, close lid, set steam release to Sealing, press the Soup button, and cook for the default time of 20 minutes.

3 When the timer beeps, quick-release the pressure and press the Cancel button. Open lid and transfer chicken to a cutting board. Shred meat with two forks and set aside.

4 In a small bowl combine water and masa, then whisk into soup. Press the Sauté button and cook, stirring constantly, until the soup has thickened, about 8 minutes. Press the Cancel button.

5 Once soup stops bubbling, stir in chicken, cheese, and sour cream and stir until the cheese is completely melted. Serve hot with tortilla chips for garnish.

PER SERVING

CALORIES: 315 | FAT: 16g | PROTEIN: 20g | SODIUM: 890mg
FIBER: 2g | CARBOHYDRATES: 18g | SUGAR: 3g

Spinach Dip Soup

Do you like spinach dip? Then you are going to love this soup! It's rich, creamy, and flavored with delicate baby spinach and savory Parmesan cheese. If you like artichoke spinach dip, add a 10-ounce jar of marinated artichokes, drained and chopped, to the soup along with the broth. Serve with butter crackers for dipping.

- **Hands-On Time: 20 minutes**
- **Cook Time: 5 minutes**

Serves 6

3 tablespoons unsalted butter

1 medium yellow onion, peeled and chopped

3 cloves garlic, peeled and minced

10 ounces baby spinach, chopped

½ teaspoon salt

½ teaspoon ground black pepper

¼ teaspoon ground nutmeg

3 cups Chicken Broth (see recipe in Chapter 2)

8 ounces cream cheese, cubed, at room temperature

1 cup heavy cream

1 cup Parmesan cheese, divided

1 Press the Sauté button on the Instant Pot® and melt butter. Add onion and cook until tender, about 5 minutes. Add garlic and baby spinach and cook until spinach is well wilted, stirring to bring wilted spinach from the bottom to the top, about 5 minutes. Add salt, pepper, and nutmeg and cook for 30 seconds.

2 Add broth and stir well. Press the Cancel button, close lid, set steam release to Sealing, press the Manual button, and set time to 5 minutes. When the timer beeps, quick-release the pressure and open lid. Stir in cream cheese, allowing it to melt fully. Add cream and ½ cup Parmesan cheese. Serve hot with remaining Parmesan for garnish.

PER SERVING

CALORIES: 772 | FAT: 72g | PROTEIN: 11g | SODIUM: 695mg
FIBER: 1g | CARBOHYDRATES: 9g | SUGAR: 3g

French Dip Soup

This soup is everything good about a French dip sandwich—tender roast beef, soft onions, melted cheese, and even the crusty bread soaked in the beefy jus. If you like, use smoked provolone cheese for extra flavor.

- **Hands-On Time: 30 minutes**
- **Cook Time: 30 minutes**

Serves 6

3 tablespoons vegetable oil

1 pound bottom round roast, cut into 3" pieces

3 medium yellow onions, peeled and sliced

4 cloves garlic, peeled and minced

1 teaspoon dried thyme

½ teaspoon dried oregano

½ teaspoon salt

½ teaspoon black pepper

½ cup sherry

3 cups Beef Broth (see recipe in Chapter 2)

1 teaspoon Worcestershire sauce

1 bay leaf

2 cups plain croutons

1 cup shredded provolone cheese

HOMEMADE CROUTONS

To make croutons, cut crusty bread into 1" pieces. Place bread on a baking sheet and coat lightly with olive oil. Season with salt and pepper, then bake at 350°F for 10–12 minutes. Cool croutons completely on the pan before using.

1 Press the Sauté button on the Instant Pot® and heat oil. Add half the beef, leaving space between each piece to avoid steaming, browning for 3 minutes per side. Transfer beef to a plate and repeat with remaining beef.

2 To pot add onions and cook until tender, about 5 minutes. Add garlic, thyme, oregano, salt, and pepper and cook until fragrant, about 1 minute. Add sherry, scraping bottom of pot well, and cool until reduced by half, about 1 minute.

3 Add browned beef, broth, Worcestershire sauce, and bay leaf to pot and stir well. Press the Cancel button, close lid, set steam release to Sealing, press the Manual button, and set time to 30 minutes.

4 When the timer beeps, let pressure release naturally, about 20 minutes. Open lid and remove bay leaf. Remove beef from pot and shred with two forks. Return to pot and stir well. Serve hot with croutons and cheese for garnish.

PER SERVING

CALORIES: 321 | **FAT:** 16g | **PROTEIN:** 25g | **SODIUM:** 681mg
FIBER: 2g | **CARBOHYDRATES:** 15g | **SUGAR:** 3g

Shrimp Paella Soup

Traditional paella is made in a large sturdy pan that allows the rice to toast on the bottom. While this soup may not have the toasted rice of the traditional, it does have all the other wonderful flavors of the Spanish classic. If you want to splurge, toss a hefty pinch (about 1/4 teaspoon) of saffron threads into the pot with the rice.

- **Hands-On Time: 15 minutes**
- **Cook Time: 4 minutes**

Serves 6

3 tablespoons salted butter

1 medium yellow onion, peeled and chopped

1 medium red bell pepper, seeded and chopped

8 ounces Spanish chorizo, chopped

3 cloves garlic, peeled and minced

1 teaspoon paprika

1 teaspoon ground turmeric

1/4 teaspoon crushed red pepper flakes

1/4 teaspoon salt

1/4 teaspoon ground black pepper

1 cup white wine

3 cups Chicken Broth (see recipe in Chapter 2)

1/2 cup uncooked white rice

1 pound medium peeled, deveined shrimp

2 scallions, thinly sliced

1 Press the Sauté button on the Instant Pot® and melt butter. Add onion and bell pepper and cook until tender, about 5 minutes. Add chorizo, garlic, paprika, turmeric, red pepper flakes, salt, and black pepper and cook until fragrant, about 1 minute. Add wine and cook, scraping bottom of pot well, until reduced by half, about 2 minutes.

2 Add broth, rice, shrimp, and scallions to pot and stir well. Press the Cancel button, close lid, set steam release to Sealing, press the Manual button, and set time to 4 minutes. When the timer beeps, quick-release the pressure and open lid. Serve hot.

PER SERVING

CALORIES: 380 | FAT: 20g | PROTEIN: 22g | SODIUM: 1,044mg
FIBER: 1g | CARBOHYDRATES: 19g | SUGAR: 2g

Chicken and Paneer Tikka Masala Soup

This soup is a take on the Indian favorite chicken tikka masala, spiced chicken in a creamy curry and tomato gravy. Cooking this spicy soup under pressure will help infuse each bite with bold flavor.

- **Hands-On Time: 15 minutes**
- **Cook Time: 20 minutes**

Serves 6

3 tablespoons coconut oil

1 medium yellow onion, peeled and chopped

3 cloves garlic, peeled and minced

2 teaspoons grated ginger

1 teaspoon garam masala

½ teaspoon ground cumin

½ teaspoon ground turmeric

¼ teaspoon ground cinnamon

¼ teaspoon salt

¼ teaspoon ground black pepper

1 (28-ounce) can crushed tomatoes

2 cups Chicken Broth (see recipe in Chapter 2)

1 pound boneless, skinless chicken breasts, cut into 1" pieces

1 (8-ounce) block paneer cheese, cut into ½" pieces

½ cup heavy cream

1 Press the Sauté button on the Instant Pot® and heat coconut oil. Add onion and cook until tender, about 5 minutes. Add garlic, ginger, garam masala, cumin, turmeric, cinnamon, salt, and pepper and cook until fragrant, about 1 minute. Press the Cancel button.

2 Add remaining ingredients to pot except paneer and cream. Stir well. Close lid, set steam release to Sealing, press the Manual button, and set time to 10 minutes. When the timer beeps, quick-release the pressure and open lid. Stir in paneer and cream. Let stand on the Keep Warm setting for 10 minutes. Serve hot.

PER SERVING

CALORIES: 392 | FAT: 24g | PROTEIN: 28g | SODIUM: 394mg
FIBER: 3g | CARBOHYDRATES: 14g | SUGAR: 8g

Eggroll Soup with Crispy Wontons

Shredded coleslaw mix has the right amount of carrot, cabbage, and often red cabbage, and takes much of the prep work out of this soup. If you prefer to shred it yourself, look for Napa cabbage instead of Savoy cabbage for a more authentic flavor.

- **Hands-On Time: 20 minutes**
- **Cook Time: 8 minutes**

Serves 6

1 tablespoon vegetable oil

1 pound ground pork

2 tablespoons hoisin sauce

1 medium yellow onion, peeled and sliced

3 cloves garlic, minced

1 tablespoon soy sauce

¼ teaspoon Chinese five-spice powder

¼ teaspoon black pepper

3 cups Chicken Broth (see recipe in Chapter 2)

1 (16-ounce) bag coleslaw mix with carrots

2 cups fried wonton strips

2 scallions, thinly sliced

1 Press the Sauté button on the Instant Pot® and heat oil. Add pork and cook, crumbling well, until browned, about 10 minutes. Add hoisin sauce and stir to coat pork, then add onion and cook until tender, about 5 minutes. Add garlic, soy sauce, Chinese five-spice, and pepper and cook until fragrant, about 1 minute.

2 Add broth and coleslaw mix to pot and stir well. Press the Cancel button, close lid, set steam release to Sealing, press the Manual button, and set time to 8 minutes.

3 When the timer beeps, quick-release the pressure.

4 Serve hot with wonton strips and scallions for garnish.

PER SERVING

CALORIES: 331 | FAT: 19g | PROTEIN: 19g | SODIUM: 382mg
FIBER: 3g | CARBOHYDRATES: 21g | SUGAR: 5g

FRYING WONTONS AT HOME

If you are unable to find fried wonton strips, you can easily make them yourself. Wonton skins are available in most grocery stores in the produce or freezer section. Cut wonton skins into ¼" strips. In a large saucepan, heat about 1" of oil to 350°F. Fry the strips, a few at a time, until golden, about 20–30 seconds. Transfer to a paper towel to drain.

International Soups

One of the joys of life is exploring the foods and cultures of people around the world. Travel can be expensive, so it is not always practical to hop on a jet and visit exotic lands. There is an easy solution for those who want to explore but also want to save for retirement: food! Making meals from distant lands is an easy and inexpensive way to enjoy flavors from around the world. If you can, take time to visit Asian, Latin, or Indian markets to source your ingredients. It can be an adventure you can enjoy close to home as you explore different ingredients, spices, and produce.

From fast-cooking soups to long-simmered stews, the Instant Pot® is your passport to a flavorful meal in much less time! For example, traditional Japanese ramen broth takes hours to prepare. In the Instant Pot® the same broth is ready in about two hours, and you get all the same bold, rich flavor.

So explore Latin America, Europe, Asia, and more with delicious soups from around the world, and save time and washing up by making them all in your Instant Pot®!

Borscht

Borscht is a popular soup in Eastern and Central Europe. You can make it with a variety of different meats and vegetables depending on your taste, but this version is based on the Russian version of the dish. Make it up to four days ahead, or freeze it for up to three months.

- **Hands-On Time: 20 minutes**
- **Cook Time: 33 minutes**

Serves 8

5 slices bacon, chopped

3 medium carrots, peeled and chopped

1 medium onion, peeled and chopped

4 cloves garlic, peeled and minced

1 (14.5-ounce) can diced tomatoes

½ teaspoon salt

½ teaspoon ground black pepper

¼ teaspoon crushed red pepper flakes

1 bay leaf

2 pounds bone-in beef short ribs

2 cups Beef Broth (see recipe in Chapter 2)

1 cup water

3 cups shredded cabbage

3 large beets, peeled and chopped

2 tablespoons white vinegar

1 cup sour cream

¼ cup chopped fresh dill

1 Press the Sauté button on the Instant Pot® and add bacon and cook until edges just start to brown and the fat starts to render, about 4 minutes. Add carrots and onion and cook until just tender, about 5 minutes, then add garlic and cook until fragrant, about 30 seconds.

2 Add tomatoes, salt, black pepper, red pepper, bay leaf, and short ribs. Add broth and stir to combine. Press the Cancel button, close lid, set steam release to Sealing, press the Manual button, and set time to 30 minutes.

3 When the timer beeps, let pressure release naturally, about 20 minutes. Open lid and transfer short ribs to a cutting board. Remove bones and gently shred meat with two forks. Return to pot along with water, cabbage, beets, and vinegar. Press the Cancel button, close lid, set steam release to Sealing, press the Manual button, and set time to 3 minutes.

4 When the timer beeps, quick-release the pressure. Open lid, discard bay leaf, and stir well. Serve hot with sour cream and dill for garnish.

PER SERVING

CALORIES: 381 | FAT: 22g | PROTEIN: 27g | SODIUM: 541mg
FIBER: 3g | CARBOHYDRATES: 12g | SUGAR: 7g

Hot and Sour Soup

Hot and Sour Soup gets its name from the white pepper and vinegar used to flavor the broth. White pepper is not so much spicy as it is hot, so the heat from the soup does not linger like that of a chili pepper but flashes across your tongue. Make this soup when you have a cold—the heat and pleasant sour flavor will be sure to make you feel better.

- **Hands-On Time: 20 minutes**
- **Cook Time: 6 minutes**

Serves 8

4 ounces boneless pork shoulder, finely minced

1 tablespoon plus ¼ cup cornstarch, divided

1 tablespoon plus ¼ cup soy sauce, divided

1 tablespoon mirin

3 teaspoons ground white pepper, divided

5 cups Chicken Broth (see recipe in Chapter 2)

1 cup water

1 cup julienned carrots

1 (8-ounce) can bamboo shoots, drained and rinsed

12 ounces shiitake mushrooms, stemmed and sliced

1 ounce dried wood ear mushrooms, soaked in hot water for 30 minutes, drained, and julienned

1 tablespoon minced garlic

2 teaspoons minced ginger

⅓ cup rice wine vinegar

1 teaspoon sugar

7 ounces medium-firm tofu, cut into cubes

2 large eggs, beaten

2 scallions, thinly sliced

2 teaspoons toasted sesame oil

1 In a large bowl combine pork, 1 tablespoon cornstarch, 1 tablespoon soy sauce, mirin, and 1 teaspoon white pepper. Mix well, then let stand for 30 minutes.

2 Add pork and marinade, broth, water, carrots, bamboo shoots, shiitake mushrooms, wood ear mushrooms, garlic, and ginger to the Instant Pot® and stir well. Close lid, set steam release to Sealing, press the Manual button, and set time to 5 minutes.

3 When the timer beeps, quick-release the pressure and open lid. In a small bowl combine remaining ¼ cup cornstarch, remaining ¼ cup soy sauce, remaining 2 teaspoons white pepper, rice vinegar, and sugar. Mix until smooth, then stir into pot and add tofu. Press the Cancel button, then press the Sauté button and cook, stirring constantly, until soup starts to thicken, about 1 minute.

4 Press the Cancel button, then slowly drizzle eggs into soup while stirring constantly to form ribbons. Serve hot, topped with scallions and a drizzle of sesame oil.

PER SERVING

CALORIES: 147 | FAT: 4g | PROTEIN: 11g | SODIUM: 614mg
FIBER: 3g | CARBOHYDRATES: 16g | SUGAR: 4g

Wonton Soup

If preparing fresh wontons feels like too much to manage, you can substitute frozen wontons from the grocery store or an Asian market. Cook them as directed, adding 2 minutes to the cooking time.

- **Hands-On Time: 35 minutes**
- **Cook Time: 11 minutes**

Serves 8

8 ounces ground pork

1 teaspoon plus ¼ cup cornstarch, divided

¼ cup soy sauce, divided

2 scallions, thinly sliced, divided

¼ teaspoon toasted sesame oil

1¼ teaspoons minced garlic, divided

1¼ teaspoons minced fresh ginger, divided

20 wonton skins

5 cups Chicken Broth (see recipe in Chapter 2)

2 baby bok choy, chopped

1 medium carrot, peeled and thinly sliced

6 ounces shiitake mushrooms, stemmed and sliced

⅓ cup water

1 In a large bowl combine pork, 1 teaspoon cornstarch, 1 teaspoon soy sauce, 1 tablespoon sliced scallion, sesame oil, ¼ teaspoon garlic, and ¼ teaspoon ginger. Mix well.

2 Place wonton skins on a work surface, then divide pork mixture among skins. Dampen a finger with water and run along one side of wonton, then fold and press to seal. Cover filled wontons with a kitchen towel and set aside.

3 Add broth, bok choy, carrot, mushrooms, and remaining soy sauce, garlic, and ginger to the Instant Pot®. Close lid, set steam release to Sealing, press the Manual button, and set time to 5 minutes.

4 When the timer beeps, quick-release the pressure, and open lid. Press the Cancel button, then press the Sauté button and drop in prepared wontons. Cook, stirring occasionally, until wontons float, about 5 minutes.

5 In a small bowl combine water and remaining ¼ cup cornstarch. Mix until smooth, then stir into pot and cook, stirring constantly, until soup starts to thicken, about 1 minute. Top with remaining scallions and serve hot.

PER SERVING

CALORIES: 196 | FAT: 5g | PROTEIN: 13g | SODIUM: 720mg
FIBER: 3g | CARBOHYDRATES: 24g | SUGAR: 3g

Egg Drop Soup

Probably the best-known soup in most Chinese restaurants, Egg Drop Soup is a popular starter to a larger meal, but it also makes a lovely entrée on its own. You can serve this soup topped with crisp wonton strips if you like, but a simple topping of green onion and sesame oil helps preserve the delicate flavor of the egg and chicken.

- **Hands-On Time: 15 minutes**
- **Cook Time: 6 minutes**

Serves 8

4 ounces boneless, skinless chicken breast, finely minced

1 tablespoon plus ¼ cup cornstarch, divided

1 tablespoon soy sauce

¼ teaspoon ground white pepper

5 cups Chicken Broth (see recipe in Chapter 2)

1 teaspoon minced garlic

1 teaspoon minced fresh ginger

⅓ cup water

½ cup frozen corn

4 large eggs, beaten

2 scallions, thinly sliced

2 teaspoons toasted sesame oil

1. In a large bowl combine chicken, 1 tablespoon cornstarch, soy sauce, and white pepper. Mix well, then let stand for 30 minutes.

2. Add chicken and marinade, broth, garlic, and ginger to pot and stir well. Close lid, set steam release to Sealing, press the Manual button, and set time to 5 minutes.

3. When the timer beeps, quick-release the pressure and open lid. In a small bowl combine water and remaining ¼ cup cornstarch. Mix until smooth, then stir into pot and add corn. Press the Cancel button, then press the Sauté button and cook, stirring constantly, until soup starts to thicken, about 1 minute.

4. Press the Cancel button, then slowly drizzle eggs into soup while stirring constantly to form ribbons. Serve hot, topped with scallions and a drizzle of sesame oil.

PER SERVING

CALORIES: 94 | FAT: 3g | PROTEIN: 8g | SODIUM: 157mg
FIBER: 0g | CARBOHYDRATES: 7g | SUGAR: 0g

Vietnamese Beef Phở

Cinnamon, ginger, star anise, and other spices are added to store-bought broth to create an authentic-tasting and speedy phở. The Instant Pot® helps extract the flavors from the spices and vegetables in a way that stove top cooking can't without hours of simmering.

- **Hands-On Time: 20 minutes**
- **Cook Time: 6 minutes**

Serves 6

1 tablespoon vegetable oil

1 medium onion, peeled and cut in half

1 (1") piece ginger, peeled and halved

6 cloves garlic, peeled and crushed

2 star anise

1 cinnamon stick

1 teaspoon coriander seeds

4 whole cloves

1 teaspoon salt

1 teaspoon whole black peppercorns

4 cups beef stock

2 tablespoons fish sauce

2 tablespoons soy sauce

1 tablespoon sugar

12 ounces rice noodles, soaked in warm water for 30 minutes and drained

½ pound cooked flank steak, thinly sliced

1 cup fresh mint leaves

1 cup fresh basil leaves

1 cup fresh bean sprouts

2 small jalapeño peppers, seeded and sliced

4 scallions, cut into 1" pieces

1 small lime, cut into wedges

1 Press the Sauté button on the Instant Pot® and heat oil. Add onion and ginger, cut sides down, to pot. Cook until onion and ginger start to brown, about 5 minutes, then remove from pot. Add garlic, star anise, cinnamon, coriander, cloves, salt, and peppercorns to pot and toast until fragrant, about 2 minutes. Return onion and ginger to pot, add stock, and stir well. Press the Cancel button.

2 Close lid, set steam release to Sealing, press the Manual button, and set time to 6 minutes. When the timer beeps, let pressure release naturally, about 20 minutes. Open lid and stir in fish sauce, soy sauce, and sugar. Strain broth through a colander lined with cheesecloth, then return broth to pot and turn on the Keep Warm setting.

3 To serve, ladle noodles into serving bowls. Top with hot broth and sliced steak. Serve with mint, basil, bean sprouts, jalapeños, scallions, and lime on the side so you and your guests can add them as desired to the soup.

PER SERVING

CALORIES: 382 | FAT: 9g | PROTEIN: 17g | SODIUM: 1,328mg
FIBER: 2g | CARBOHYDRATES: 54g | SUGAR: 4g

Vietnamese Chicken Phở

Dark-meat chicken offers the richest flavor, but you can use chicken breasts if you prefer. Be sure to use bone-in chicken. It adds more flavor and keeps the meat moist.

- **Hands-On Time: 20 minutes**
- **Cook Time: 6 minutes**

Serves 6

1 tablespoon vegetable oil

1 medium onion, peeled and cut in half

1 (1") piece ginger, peeled

6 cloves garlic, crushed

¼ cup chopped cilantro

1 medium Fuji apple, peeled, cored, and diced

2 star anise

3 cardamom pods, crushed

1 cinnamon stick

1 teaspoon coriander seeds

2 whole cloves

1 teaspoon salt

1 teaspoon whole black peppercorns

4 cups Chicken Stock (see recipe in Chapter 2)

1 pound bone-in, skin-on chicken thighs

2 tablespoons fish sauce

2 tablespoons soy sauce

1 tablespoon sugar

12 ounces rice noodles, soaked in warm water for 30 minutes and drained

½ pound cooked flank steak, thinly sliced

1 cup fresh mint leaves

1 cup fresh basil leaves

1 cup fresh bean sprouts

2 small jalapeño peppers, seeded and sliced

4 scallions, cut into 1" pieces

1 Press the Sauté button on the Instant Pot® and heat oil. Add onion and ginger, cut sides down, to pot. Cook until onion and ginger start to brown, about 5 minutes, then remove from pot. Add garlic, cilantro, apple, star anise, cardamom, cinnamon, coriander, cloves, salt, and peppercorns to pot and toast until fragrant, about 2 minutes. Return onion and ginger to pot, add stock and stir well. Add chicken thighs to pot. Press the Cancel button.

2 Close lid, set steam release to Sealing, press the Manual button, and set time to 6 minutes. When the timer beeps, let pressure release naturally, about 20 minutes. Open lid and stir in fish sauce, soy sauce, and sugar. Transfer chicken thighs to cutting board. Remove skin from chicken and cut meat from bones. Set aside. Strain broth through a colander lined with cheesecloth, then return broth to pot and turn on the Keep Warm setting.

3 To serve, ladle noodles into serving bowls. Top noodles with chicken, hot broth, and sliced steak. Serve with mint, basil, bean sprouts, jalapeños, and scallions on the side so you and your guests can add them as desired to the soup.

PER SERVING

CALORIES: 466 | FAT: 11g | PROTEIN: 30g | SODIUM: 1,380mg
FIBER: 3g | CARBOHYDRATES: 57g | SUGAR: 7g

Shoyu Ramen

Making ramen at home can be a multiday affair, preparing sauces, curing meat, and simmering broths for hours on end. Sometimes you just want a quick, tasty bowl of ramen, and this recipe gets you there in a flash thanks to the Instant Pot®.

- **Hands-On Time: 25 minutes**
- **Cook Time: 17 minutes**

Serves 8

2 tablespoons vegetable oil

2 pounds boneless, skinless chicken thighs

2 medium carrots, peeled and sliced

2 medium onions, peeled and chopped

6 cloves garlic, peeled and crushed

1 (2") piece fresh ginger, peeled and chopped

¼ cup light soy sauce

4 cups Chicken Stock (see recipe in Chapter 2)

1 cup water

4 (3-ounce) packages ramen noodles, seasoning packet discarded

8 scallions, cut into 1" pieces

4 large hard-cooked eggs, peeled and cut in half

8 (3") sheets toasted nori

4 teaspoons chili oil

1 Press the Sauté button on the Instant Pot® and heat oil. Add half the chicken in an even layer, making sure there is space between each piece to avoid steaming. Brown each side well, about 4 minutes per side. Transfer to a plate and repeat with remaining chicken.

2 Add carrots and onions to pot and cook until tender, about 8 minutes, then add garlic, ginger, and soy sauce and cook until fragrant, about 30 seconds. Press the Cancel button and add chicken thighs with any juices, stock, and water to pot. Stir well. Close lid, set steam release to Sealing, press the Manual button, and set time to 15 minutes.

3 When the timer beeps, quick-release the pressure and open lid. Transfer chicken to a cutting board and cut into bite-sized pieces. Return chicken to pot and add ramen noodles. Press the Cancel button, then press the Sauté button and cook until noodles are tender, about 2 minutes. Press the Cancel button and stir in scallions.

4 Serve ramen in bowls with eggs, nori, and chili oil for garnish.

PER SERVING

CALORIES: 442 | FAT: 19g | PROTEIN: 32g | SODIUM: 1,351mg
FIBER: 3g | CARBOHYDRATES: 31g | SUGAR: 3g

Tonkotsu Ramen

In Japanese *tonkotsu* translates to "pork bone broth." The broth of this ramen is cloudy from the pork bones that are slowly cooked to release all their flavor. This ramen takes a little more time than other soups, but it is totally worth it for the flavor you will achieve.

- **Hands-On Time: 15 minutes**
- **Cook Time: 2 hours**

Serves 8

2 pounds pork spare ribs, cut into 1" pieces (ask your butcher to do this for you)

2 pounds chicken bones

4 quarts water, divided

1 tablespoon vegetable oil

2 medium onions, peeled and roughly chopped

6 cloves garlic, peeled and crushed

1 (2") piece fresh ginger, peeled and chopped

1 (12-ounce) package fresh ramen noodles

8 scallions, cut into 1" pieces

4 medium boiled eggs, sliced in half

8 (3") sheets toasted nori

4 teaspoons chili oil

1 Place pork and chicken bones in the Instant Pot® pot and add 2 quarts water, making sure not to exceed the Max Fill line. Press the Sauté button and allow mixture to come just to a boil, about 30 minutes. Press the Cancel button, strain bones into a colander, and rinse the bones well under cold water. Set aside.

2 Clean out pot and dry well. Return to machine, press the Sauté button, and heat oil. Add onions and cook until tender, about 4 minutes, then add garlic and ginger and cook until fragrant, about 1 minute. Press the Cancel button.

3 Add reserved water, making sure not to exceed the Max Fill line. Close lid, set steam release to Sealing, press the Manual button, and set time to 90 minutes.

4 When the timer beeps, let pressure release naturally, about 20 minutes. Press the Cancel button. Let broth cool for 30 minutes, then strain through a colander lined with cheesecloth.

5 Return strained broth to pot and press the Sauté button. Add ramen noodles and cook according to package directions. Press the Cancel button and stir in scallions. Serve ramen in bowls with eggs, nori, and chili oil for garnish.

PER SERVING

CALORIES: 209 | FAT: 7g | PROTEIN: 9g | SODIUM: 211mg
FIBER: 2g | CARBOHYDRATES: 27g | SUGAR: 2g

Tofu and Mushroom Ramen

Fresh shiitake mushrooms and soy sauce give this ramen a balanced umami, or savory, flavor, without using any meat. For a vegan version, look for egg-free fresh ramen noodles at the Asian market, or replace the noodles with finely shredded Napa cabbage.

- **Hands-On Time: 15 minutes**
- **Cook Time: 6 minutes**

Serves 8

2 tablespoons vegetable oil

2 medium carrots, peeled and sliced

2 medium onions, peeled and chopped

18 ounces fresh shiitake mushrooms, stemmed and sliced

6 cloves garlic, peeled and crushed

1 (2") piece fresh ginger, peeled and chopped

¼ cup light soy sauce

4 cups Vegetable Broth (see recipe in Chapter 2)

1 (14-ounce) block firm tofu, drained and cubed

1 (12-ounce) package fresh ramen noodles

8 scallions, cut into 1" pieces

8 (3") sheets toasted nori

4 teaspoons chili oil

1 Press the Sauté button on the Instant Pot® and heat oil. Add carrots and onions to pot and cook until tender, about 8 minutes. Add mushrooms and cook until they just soften, about 3 minutes, then add garlic, ginger, and soy sauce and cook until fragrant, about 30 seconds. Press the Cancel button and add broth and tofu to pot. Stir well. Close lid, set steam release to Sealing, press the Manual button, and set time to 6 minutes.

2 When the timer beeps, quick-release the pressure. Open lid and add ramen noodles. Cook according to package directions. Press the Cancel button and stir in scallions. Serve ramen in bowls with nori and chili oil for garnish.

PER SERVING

CALORIES: 260 | FAT: 9g | PROTEIN: 12g | SODIUM: 635mg FIBER: 4g | CARBOHYDRATES: 34g | SUGAR: 5g

Tom Yum

Tom Yum soup is a Thai hot and sour soup made with meat and vegetables. While this recipe calls for sliced button mushrooms, straw or oyster mushrooms are more authentic and can be swapped in equal amounts.

- **Hands-On Time: 10 minutes**
- **Cook Time: 20 minutes**

Serves 6

1 tablespoon vegetable oil

1 medium white onion, peeled and thinly sliced

3 cloves garlic, peeled and minced

1 tablespoon fresh minced ginger

1 medium carrot, peeled and diced

8 ounces sliced button mushrooms

8 ounces skinless, boneless chicken breast, thinly sliced

2 scallions, thinly sliced

2 Roma tomatoes, seeded and cut into ½" pieces

8 cups Chicken Broth (see recipe in Chapter 2)

2 tablespoons lime juice

1 stalk lemongrass, chopped, or 1 tablespoon lemongrass paste

2 teaspoons fish sauce

¼ cup chopped fresh cilantro

1 teaspoon chili oil

1 Press the Sauté button on the Instant Pot® and heat oil. Add onion and cook until just tender, about 5 minutes. Add garlic and ginger and cook until fragrant, about 30 seconds. Press the Cancel button.

2 Add carrot, mushrooms, chicken, scallions, tomatoes, broth, lime juice, lemongrass, fish sauce, cilantro, and chili oil to pot and stir well. Close lid, set steam release to Sealing, press the Soup button, and cook for the default time of 20 minutes. When the timer beeps, let pressure release naturally, about 20 minutes. Open lid and stir well. Serve hot.

PER SERVING

CALORIES: 135 | FAT: 5g | PROTEIN: 13g | SODIUM: 197mg
FIBER: 2g | CARBOHYDRATES: 8g | SUGAR: 3g

Tom Kha Gai

Galangal is commonly available in Asian markets and resembles ginger, but has a smoother, paler skin. If you are unable to find it, use fresh ginger. Powdered galangal is also available, but fresh ginger's brighter flavor makes it a better substitute.

- **Hands-On Time: 10 minutes**
- **Cook Time: 20 minutes**

Serves 6

1 tablespoon vegetable oil

1 medium white onion, peeled and chopped

4 cloves garlic, peeled and minced

1 tablespoon minced fresh galangal

8 ounces sliced button mushrooms

8 ounces boneless, skinless chicken breast, thinly sliced

2 scallions, thinly sliced

6 cups Chicken Broth (see recipe in Chapter 2)

1 (15-ounce) can full-fat coconut milk

1 tablespoon lime juice

1 stalk lemongrass, chopped, or 1 tablespoon lemongrass paste

2 teaspoons fish sauce

¼ cup chopped fresh cilantro

1 teaspoon chili oil

1 Press the Sauté button on the Instant Pot® and heat oil. Add onion and cook until just tender, about 5 minutes. Add garlic and galangal and cook until fragrant, about 30 seconds. Press the Cancel button.

2 Add mushrooms, chicken, scallions, broth, coconut milk, lime juice, lemongrass, fish sauce, cilantro, and chili oil to pot and stir well. Close lid, set steam release to Sealing, press the Soup button, and cook for the default time of 20 minutes. When the timer beeps, let pressure release naturally, about 20 minutes. Open lid and stir well. Serve hot.

PER SERVING

CALORIES: 256 | FAT: 19g | PROTEIN: 14g | SODIUM: 194mg
FIBER: 1g | CARBOHYDRATES: 7g | SUGAR: 2g

Caldo de Res

Caldo de Res is a rustic Mexican beef soup. Traditionally bone-in beef is simmered on the stove until tender, then vegetables are added and it is simmered again. This version uses boneless chuck roast, and while it is still cooked in two stages, the Instant Pot® will have you tucking into a hearty bowl of soup in under an hour!

- **Hands-On Time: 10 minutes**
- **Cook Time: 25 minutes**

Serves 6

2 pounds beef chuck roast, cut into 1" pieces

2 medium carrots, peeled and roughly chopped

1 medium white onion, peeled and chopped

1 stalk celery, sliced

2 teaspoons ground cumin

½ teaspoon salt

5 cups Beef Broth (see recipe in Chapter 2)

1 medium chayote squash, peeled and chopped

1 medium ear corn, husked and cut into 1" pieces

1 medium zucchini, roughly chopped

½ head of cabbage, cored and roughly chopped

¼ cup roughly chopped cilantro

1. Add beef, carrots, onion, celery, cumin, salt, and broth to the Instant Pot® and stir well. Close lid, set steam release to Sealing, press the Soup button, and cook for the default time of 20 minutes.

2. When the timer beeps, let pressure release naturally, about 15 minutes, then press the Cancel button. Remove lid and add remaining ingredients. Close lid, set steam release to Sealing, press the Manual button, and set time to 5 minutes. When the timer beeps, quick-release the pressure. Serve hot.

PER SERVING

CALORIES: 286 | FAT: 7g | PROTEIN: 38g | SODIUM: 526mg
FIBER: 4g | CARBOHYDRATES: 15g | SUGAR: 7g

Caldo Verde

This version of the popular Portuguese soup gets its green color from kale, but you can also use collard greens if you like. If you can find it, use Portuguese chouriço sausage in place of the Spanish-style chorizo. Don't use Mexican chorizo—its soft, crumbled texture is not right for this soup.

- **Hands-On Time: 10 minutes**
- **Cook Time: 6 minutes**

Serves 6

3 tablespoons olive oil

12 ounces Spanish chorizo, sliced

4 cups chopped kale

6 medium Yukon Gold potatoes, cut into 1" pieces

1 medium white onion, peeled and chopped

1 clove garlic, peeled and minced

½ teaspoon salt

½ teaspoon ground black pepper

1 bay leaf

5 cups water

1 Press the Sauté button on the Instant Pot® and heat oil. Add chorizo and cook until edges of sausage start to brown, about 5 minutes. Drain off excess fat and return pot to machine. Add kale and turn to mix with chorizo, then add potatoes, onion, garlic, salt, pepper, bay leaf, and water and stir well. Press the Cancel button.

2 Close lid, set steam release to Sealing, press the Manual button, and adjust time to 6 minutes. When the timer beeps, let pressure release naturally, about 15 minutes. Remove lid and discard bay leaf. Serve hot.

PER SERVING

CALORIES: 426 | FAT: 23g | PROTEIN: 15g | SODIUM: 792mg
FIBER: 6g | CARBOHYDRATES: 37g | SUGAR: 3g

Frijoles a la Charra (Pinto Bean Soup)

Also called *charro beans*, this soup is popular as an appetizer or a side dish served with grilled beef or chicken. For *frijoles borrachos*, or "drunken beans," just swap out half the water with your favorite ale or lager beer.

- **Hands-On Time: 15 minutes**
- **Cook Time: 30 minutes**

Serves 8

½ pound bacon, chopped

1 large white onion, peeled and chopped

2 cloves garlic, peeled and minced

1 small jalapeño pepper, seeded and minced

2 teaspoons ground cumin

1 teaspoon ground coriander

½ teaspoon smoked paprika

1 pound pinto beans, soaked overnight and drained

4 cups water

¼ cup roughly chopped cilantro

½ teaspoon salt

1 Press the Sauté button on the Instant Pot® and add bacon. Cook, stirring often, until bacon is browned and the fat has completely rendered, about 5 minutes. Add onion and cook, stirring often, until tender, about 5 minutes.

2 Add garlic, jalapeño, cumin, coriander, and paprika and cook until the garlic and spices are fragrant, about 2 minutes. Press the Cancel button. Add beans, water, and cilantro to pot and stir well.

3 Close lid, set steam release to Sealing, press the Bean button, and cook for the default time of 30 minutes. When the timer beeps, let pressure release naturally, about 15 minutes. Remove lid, season with salt, and serve hot.

PER SERVING

CALORIES: 324 | FAT: 11g | PROTEIN: 16g | SODIUM: 341mg
FIBER: 9g | CARBOHYDRATES: 38g | SUGAR: 2g

Avgolemono

This Greek-style lemon chicken soup, thickened with egg, has a light, fresh flavor and truly lets the simplicity of the ingredients shine.

- **Hands-On Time: 10 minutes**
- **Cook Time: 17 minutes**

Serves 6

6 cups Chicken Stock (see recipe in Chapter 2)

½ cup long-grain white rice

3 cups cooked and shredded chicken breast

½ teaspoon salt

½ teaspoon black pepper

¼ cup lemon juice

2 large eggs

2 tablespoons chopped dill

1 tablespoon chopped parsley

1 Place stock and rice in the Instant Pot®. Close lid, set steam release to Sealing, press the Manual button, and adjust time to 7 minutes. When the timer beeps, quick-release the pressure. Open lid and stir in chicken, salt, and pepper.

2 In a medium bowl combine lemon and eggs, then slowly add 1 cup hot cooking liquid while constantly whisking. Add egg mixture to soup and stir. Let stand on the Keep Warm setting, stirring occasionally, for 10 minutes. Add dill and parsley. Serve hot.

PER SERVING

CALORIES: 218 | **FAT:** 5g | **PROTEIN:** 27g | **SODIUM:** 278mg
FIBER: 0g | **CARBOHYDRATES:** 13g | **SUGAR:** 0g

Kohlsuppe

This soup is basically everything good about fall in one bowl.

- **Hands-On Time: 20 minutes**
- **Cook Time: 20 minutes**

Serves 6

2 tablespoons unsalted butter

12 ounces smoked sausage, sliced

2 medium leeks, white part only, chopped

¾ cup chopped carrots

3 cups chopped cabbage

2 russet potatoes, peeled and cut into 1" pieces

1 bay leaf

4 cups Chicken Broth (see recipe in Chapter 2)

1 cup water

1 Press the Sauté button on the Instant Pot® and melt butter. Add sausage and cook until lightly browned, about 5 minutes. Add leeks, carrots, and cabbage. Cook, stirring until vegetables are just tender, about 8 minutes. Press the Cancel button.

2 Add remaining ingredients to pot. Close lid, set steam release to Sealing, press the Soup button, and cook for the default time of 20 minutes. When the timer beeps, let pressure release naturally, about 20 minutes. Open lid, discard bay leaf, and serve hot.

PER SERVING

CALORIES: 332 | **FAT:** 19g | **PROTEIN:** 11g | **SODIUM:** 697mg
FIBER: 5g | **CARBOHYDRATES:** 26g | **SUGAR:** 6g

Cock-a-Leekie Soup

This soup is best known as Scotland's national soup, but its origins are actually French. Barley is used to thicken the soup, and to make it more filling. This winter warmer is a simple, wholesome soup that is a full meal alone but is even better with hearty bread and salted butter on the side.

- **Hands-On Time: 15 minutes**
- **Cook Time: 1 hour**

Serves 6

1 (4-pound) chicken, cut into 8 pieces

4 slices thick-cut bacon, chopped

4 cups Chicken Broth (see recipe in Chapter 2)

1 tablespoon dried thyme

1 bay leaf

2 cups water

¾ cup pearl barley

4 medium leeks, white part only, chopped

2 medium carrots, peeled and chopped

½ teaspoon salt

½ teaspoon ground black pepper

3 tablespoons chopped fresh flat-leaf parsley

1 Place chicken, bacon, broth, thyme, and bay leaf in the Instant Pot®. Add water, making sure not to fill past the Max Fill line. Close lid, set steam release to Sealing, press the Manual button, and set time to 30 minutes.

2 When the timer beeps, quick-release the pressure and press the Cancel button. Carefully transfer chicken to a cutting board and allow to cool. Remove meat from bones and shred. Set aside. Discard skin and bones.

3 To pot add barley, leeks, and carrots. Close lid, set steam release to Sealing, press the Manual button, and set time to 20 minutes.

4 When the timer beeps, quick-release the pressure. Open lid and return chicken to pot, then let stand on the Keep Warm setting for 10 minutes. Discard bay leaf. Add salt and pepper and garnish with chopped parsley.

PER SERVING

CALORIES: 426 | FAT: 16g | PROTEIN: 36g | SODIUM: 451mg
FIBER: 6g | CARBOHYDRATES: 30g | SUGAR: 4g

Mulligatawny Soup

Mulligatawny soup originates from South India, but is also very popular in the United Kingdom. The version that most people know today is a version of the original Indian dish with British modifications. It's a pub menu staple, served with pints of dark beer and crusty bread for dipping. Try it garnished with a little sour cream.

- **Hands-On Time: 20 minutes**
- **Cook Time: 20 minutes**

Serves 6

2 tablespoons ghee

4 large carrots, peeled and finely diced

2 stalks celery, finely diced

1 medium yellow onion, peeled and diced

2 cloves garlic, peeled and minced

½ teaspoon garam masala

½ teaspoon ground turmeric

½ teaspoon ground coriander

¼ teaspoon crushed red pepper flakes

½ teaspoon ground cumin

½ teaspoon ground cardamom

½ teaspoon ground ginger

½ teaspoon salt

½ teaspoon freshly cracked black pepper

1 pound boneless, skinless chicken thighs, cut into ½" pieces

4 cups Chicken Broth (see recipe in Chapter 2)

2 cups water

1 cup red lentils

¼ cup chopped fresh cilantro

1 Press the Sauté button on the Instant Pot® and heat ghee. Add carrots, celery, and onion. Cook until tender, about 8 minutes, then add garlic, garam masala, turmeric, coriander, red pepper flakes, cumin, cardamom, ginger, salt, and pepper. Cook until spices and garlic are fragrant, about 1 minute.

2 Add chicken, broth, and water and stir well, then add lentils and mix to combine. Press the Cancel button. Close lid, set steam release to Sealing, press the Soup button, and cook for the default time of 20 minutes.

3 When the timer beeps, let pressure release naturally, about 20 minutes. Open lid, add cilantro, and stir well. Serve hot.

PER SERVING

CALORIES: 292 | **FAT:** 9g | **PROTEIN:** 25g | **SODIUM:** 317mg
FIBER: 6g | **CARBOHYDRATES:** 28g | **SUGAR:** 3g

US/Metric Conversion Chart

VOLUME CONVERSIONS

US Volume Measure	Metric Equivalent
⅛ teaspoon	0.5 milliliter
¼ teaspoon	1 milliliter
½ teaspoon	2 milliliters
1 teaspoon	5 milliliters
½ tablespoon	7 milliliters
1 tablespoon (3 teaspoons)	15 milliliters
2 tablespoons (1 fluid ounce)	30 milliliters
¼ cup (4 tablespoons)	60 milliliters
⅓ cup	90 milliliters
½ cup (4 fluid ounces)	125 milliliters
⅔ cup	160 milliliters
¾ cup (6 fluid ounces)	180 milliliters
1 cup (16 tablespoons)	250 milliliters
1 pint (2 cups)	500 milliliters
1 quart (4 cups)	1 liter (about)

WEIGHT CONVERSIONS

US Weight Measure	Metric Equivalent
½ ounce	15 grams
1 ounce	30 grams
2 ounces	60 grams
3 ounces	85 grams
¼ pound (4 ounces)	115 grams
½ pound (8 ounces)	225 grams
¾ pound (12 ounces)	340 grams
1 pound (16 ounces)	454 grams

OVEN TEMPERATURE CONVERSIONS

Degrees Fahrenheit	Degrees Celsius
200 degrees F	95 degrees C
250 degrees F	120 degrees C
275 degrees F	135 degrees C
300 degrees F	150 degrees C
325 degrees F	160 degrees C
350 degrees F	180 degrees C
375 degrees F	190 degrees C
400 degrees F	205 degrees C
425 degrees F	220 degrees C
450 degrees F	230 degrees C

BAKING PAN SIZES

American	Metric
8 x 1½ inch round baking pan	20 x 4 cm cake tin
9 x 1½ inch round baking pan	23 x 3.5 cm cake tin
11 x 7 x 1½ inch baking pan	28 x 18 x 4 cm baking tin
13 x 9 x 2 inch baking pan	30 x 20 x 5 cm baking tin
2 quart rectangular baking dish	30 x 20 x 3 cm baking tin
15 x 10 x 2 inch baking pan	30 x 25 x 2 cm baking tin (Swiss roll tin)
9 inch pie plate	22 x 4 or 23 x 4 cm pie plate
7 or 8 inch springform pan	18 or 20 cm springform or loose bottom cake tin
9 x 5 x 3 inch loaf pan	23 x 13 x 7 cm or 2 lb narrow loaf or pâté tin
1½ quart casserole	1.5 liter casserole
2 quart casserole	2 liter casserole

Index